Under A-Rest

Paul Hedderman

Book composed/written through transcribed talks by Julie Rumbarger. Edited and overseen by Paul Hedderman with Monique Kuster-Janes and Julie Rumbarger. Book Cover by Michael Dowdall.

Paul's message in AA and Non-Duality can be found at zenbitchslap.com

Index

This book is dedicated to Jim Cook.
He is peace, resting.

The Dilemma

The Solution has nothing to do with the problem.

I'd say my golden years were between the ages of two and four. When I was playing, that's all that I was doing was playing. I wasn't thinking about playing next week because time hadn't set in yet. I wasn't thinking that I could be anywhere else because I hadn't entertained that possibility. What you might call 'being in the moment,' was just the norm.

What occurred was I outgrew that state of mind. There was sort of a brightness to it, a sense of an immediacy and spontaneity that I outgrew. I started to grow into introspection where it seemed that my attention and interest went to the thought stream instead of the living of the day. This provoked an irritability, restlessness and discontent that built as I kept getting older. I was rooted in this negative feeling of wrongness and who I thought I was.

As an example, I remember being eleven years old and I was going through the hallway at school when a pretty girl said hello to me. I went home and wondered what she meant by it for about five hours. I was in the throes of being obsessed with self where everything was very profound. The days of just walking into a room unaccompanied by thought were over. Everything was thought about. Everything was being seen as how it pertained to me. It produced a restlessness that demanded relief. I wasn't finding any relief through sports or other activities.

One night when I was about eleven or twelve years old, I was at a little league game. It was a night game and my mother had not come so I was going to walk home by myself. After the game, a guy came into the dugout with two six-packs of beer. I had my first drink of alcohol and my athletic career came to a screeching halt. I had found what I was looking for. I didn't know what I was looking for, but when I had that first beer I knew I had found it; relief from alcoholism. Drinking alcohol was my first solution to alcoholism. From that point on, I wanted that relief and I started to chase it.

As soon as I started drinking I had a realization that I had a magnetic appeal to people in uniform. I started to experience the consequences of my drinking and ended up getting arrested. The arrests were getting more and more grave as time went on. By the time I hit 16 years old, I was kicked out of school and dealing drugs out of my mother's house.

We lived in a two-family home in Long Island. We were the family on the bottom floor. There was a cellar and in that cellar was a room that I made my little "office". I painted it red and put up these cut-out moons and stars that would shine in the dark. From there I was selling drugs. I didn't know that my house was under surveillance.

After a few months of "doing business," I was sitting in my room with seven guys, tripping on LSD, watching a construction light blinking on and off and listening to a Jimi Hendrix song, "Third Stone to the Sun," which if you played it slow, he talked as an alien visiting our planet. It captured perfectly our collective states of mind.

I had 1000 hits of LSD in the room when the police raided the house. It was my first big, major arrest. This set off trains of circumstances that brought me misfortune that I felt I didn't deserve, yet this and all the other misfortunes that followed proved unable to bring me to my senses. I kept doing the same things hoping for different results but they always led to the same condition, "I'm screwed." In hindsight I realized that every time I drank I didn't get in trouble, but every time I got in trouble, I was drinking.

My life kept spiraling downward. By the time I reached my thirties, I ended up in San Francisco in a drug and alcohol program called Delancey Street. I walked into the building where they had a bench that when you sit on it, signifies that you had lost the game of life and you were coming over to the sidelines to get some help, but I was in the throes of this little video in my head of "Paul." When anything ever happened to me, it was like me portraying the person it was happening to. I was very disengaged from my own life. I looked at the clock on the wall, it was 6:00. Well dressed clients were walking by looking very busy. I said to myself, "I'm going to give these people till 6:30 or I'm out of here," like I had a lot of important engagements to keep. I had nowhere to go. I didn't have a pot to piss in. By 6:28, they brought me into a room and interviewed me. They said one thing which I was very keen on, "Do you want a place to stay tonight?" That's what I really needed, I needed a place to stay. They said I had to make a two-year commitment and I gulped, but decided "Sure, I'll stay here for two years," with absolutely no intention of staying there for more than a night.

They accepted me, and by 6:35 I was a full-fledged member of Delancey Street which had three hundred clients running around. They released me into the mass population and what was amazing was Delancey Street proved to be a big enough buffer between me and me. I actually thrived and stayed sober for the two years that I was there. I stayed the whole two years. I'm not really proud of it, but I actually do great in an institutional setting. I do pretty good when people are telling me what to do.

I was living 24 hours a day, the Delancey Street way. I wasn't asking much council. It had nothing to do with what I would call a Spiritual program yet it was doing me a lot of good. You work six days a week and if you did anything wrong you were punished. That was sufficient to keep me at bay, so to speak.

After about a year, I came to the conclusion that my problem was narcotics but thought I could probably drink. I didn't run this by anyone in the facility, I just stored it in my head and continued with the program.

At the 20-month mark, I had a decision to make. They asked me if I would want to stay five more years in the program and if not I could enter the workout program. The workout program is where you get a job and work for four months and if you fulfill a few requirements, you can graduate and you'll be done. I went for the latter. I agreed to the four month workout. I had to get a job, which I did, driving a little step van, delivering hardware. I had to open up a checking account, which I did. I had to get a car, which I did. I was working for four months and they were helping me save my money. At the four month mark, the next thing I needed to do was find a place to live outside of Delancey Street. I started to look around San Francisco and I found a really nice place that was affordable. I really wanted the place but there were like 20 applicants looking to get it. At this point I looked pretty good. I had khaki pants, a blue blazer and I hadn't been drinking or using for two years.

I like to say my realtor was Dr. Jekyll. They liked Dr. Jekyll but Mr. Hyde was going to be moving in, unbeknownst to myself. Delancey Street told me that though the Mr. Hyde period was rather long, it was now over; I was going to be Dr. Jekyll from now on. I was hoping they were right but I had a strong suspicion that they may be wrong.

I got the place as Dr. Jekyll, but as soon as I left Delancey Street, the irritability, restlessness and discontent (the base of alcoholism) overcame me and called forth the emergence of Mr. Hyde. After I got home from work, I didn't know what to do with myself. It seemed like an eternity from the time I got home till 11 o'clock when I would go to bed. I couldn't handle the responsibility of how to fill my own time. I had gotten used to being told what to do.

That night, sitting in my room, the advertising started to occur in my head. It started to tell me what I had been missing for the last two years, like all of these incredible great times. The mental report was not fact based. It didn't tell me specifically what I was missing, like getting shot at, run over by cars or getting arrested. It made it more mythical, frolicking and romantic. I fell for it.

I got into my little Toyota Corolla and I drove to a bar, the first time in two years. It was called *The Rose and Thistle*, we used to call it the nose and sniffle. I walked in armed with this idea that I can drink. I sat down at the bar and being obsessed with this idea of me, I thought the bartender had been getting my newsletter and that he wouldn't serve me, but I put the money down and he gave me a beer. The first one in two years. Nothing happened. It seemed I had impunity.

The AA police didn't rush in, no one even turned around to look. I ordered a second beer and half way through the second beer--it's not enough for me. I want *more*. (Whatever you think more is, just fill in the blank) I looked around the bar to see if there was anyone selling more and the same guy that used to sell more there, was still there like he had a franchise. I bought some more and I went out to my Toyota Corolla that I was going to lose in two days, and I did a line of more.

As soon as I did the line of more it was like that movie, *The Shining,* with Jack Nicholson when he comes through the door at the end and says, "Here's Johnny." It was just like that.

I was possessed and I went on a ten-month run from that night on. If you have ever been on a run, you know that title "run" is quite misleading. You start running but soon you're limping, then crawling, then dragged back to that state we call pitiful and incomprehensible demoralization. I forgot all about the college I attended while in Delancey Street.

I lost the job. Everything just fell away and I was taken over by the mental parasite called alcoholism. I had two years of health so it took ten months, but I ended up at a bottom again. Every time I landed on a bottom, I just moved in, put curtains up and invited people over. The problem was, no matter how low the bottom was, I kept getting evicted from that bottom and going to a new lower one.

After ten months of running around like this, I went on an adventure on St. Patrick's Day, March 17th, 1988, and ended up March 20th, in a town about two hours north of San Francisco. I found myself in a trailer park with a guy I didn't know, watching a cowboy movie and drinking a bottle of Royal Gate vodka--a very fine quality vodka, about $0.90 a pint. In my circle, the gate you always entered near the end is the Royal Gate. We were passing the bottle of vodka back and forth while waiting for a mutual acquaintance, hoping someone would have money so we could get more. I didn't know this dude, I just found myself sitting there with him. I looked at him, he was a heavy guy with a bulbous nose and varicose veins on his face and I said to myself, "Man, this guy is a bum," but lo and behold, he looked at me like I was a bum.

Suddenly, my head *stopped and like lightning* flashing across a screen, a news flash suddenly appeared, no story, just a headline, "I'm Screwed." This pierced the innermost of what I am. That driving force of alcoholism, that imperative, that need to get out of myself through whatever means necessary or available was suspended. Something that I didn't even know was possible had been done. Until this point, no human power could relieve me of this alcoholism. I wanted to stop, my mother wanted me to stop, the state wanted me to stop.

Nothing could bring about what was so freely done in that moment. Everyone who knew me, knew I had been screwed for quite a while but it was like news to me; it stopped me in my tracks. I didn't reach for the vodka and I started to have new thoughts that I wasn't even close to having two minutes before.

I got up and went to a phone booth and called Delancey Street. I asked if they would take me back. They had been getting my newsletter and they basically said, "No, you can't come back right now, you can come back in a month and we'll interview you again and maybe we'll take you, maybe we won't."

The portal that opened up and whatever came through had brought honesty with it and I said the first honest thing I'd said in ten months which was, "Hey, I don't think I have a month." I got off the phone and called a woman I used to party with in the city and I must have sounded humble enough because she bought into what I was saying. I asked her if she could help me and give me a ride back to the city. I told her that I was done. She'd always wanted to help me, so she drove up. It took about an hour and a half. In that hour and a half I had a miraculous alcoholic recovery and I wanted to get loaded again. I forgot all about the portal and the moment of clarity; I just wanted to get high. But really what I wanted to do was escape from self.

She came up and I got in the car and started trying to talk her into buying a six pack of talls, get the drugs, the dirty magazines and rent a hotel room but she followed that equation with me many times before. It hadn't been that satisfying for her. She said no. She asked me if I wanted a place to stay which was what I wanted. She said that I had to go to a recovery meeting. This offer sounded incredibly different than the deal that was made two years and ten months before where I had to make a two year commitment for that one night of sanctuary. She said to just go to a meeting for one hour and then I could stay at her house. I said sure.

She brought me to my first meeting--March 21st, 1988. I have been sober and clean since then.

Grace

In my case, I didn't come to AA based on a bottom, I really believe that I came to AA based on Grace because I was just gonna keep on keepin' on until I was either dead, institutionalized again, or in jail. I had no intention. I had really come to accept the destiny of my life which was to just keep trying to get loaded until something stops me. The bottoms never provoked sobriety for me, something more was needed, a divine intervention.

For me it was a moment of Grace. My whole program is based on Grace because when I went to her house and finally got to sleep, the miracle happened. When I woke up the next day, that imperative to get high, to get loaded, had dimmed down and some other thoughts took its place which were: "I'd better call this program, this *Alcoholics Anonymous* and find out if there's a meeting earlier than eight o'clock at night because I'm not going to make it till eight o'clock at night."

I went to a meeting at noon that day. I've been going to meetings and staying in our community for the last 29 years.

What I find initiates the psychic change for me is Grace. What fills the psychic change is Grace and one way the Grace can come through in an alcoholic's life is through the 12 steps of recovery.

This action figure's managing always led me to having to be managed by others. I feel I am always led by something, be it the mental state or Spirit.

The effects of being led depends on what is leading. In my experience, living a life based on the mental interpretation is encapsulated in the form of looking called self-centeredness that perceives, 'life is happening to me'. The sense of being led by something other than the mental state is seeing 'life is happening'. Faith in one overrides the influence of the other.

What is presented in this writing is not of my making. It's the influence of a power greater than self that has been able to access through me, into life, through the steps in the program of *Alcoholics Anonymous.*

The *Big Book* of *Alcoholics Anonymous*, in the forward, makes a simple statement: "*We are more than 100 men and women who have recovered from a seemingly hopeless state of mind and body.*"

One definition of the word seemingly is that things appear to be true or false to us. In the throes of the disease, I am in a hopeless state of mind and body but when I start to recover I realize it was a seemingly state of mind and body. It really points out our role in things, that how things appear is how they appear **to us**. It's very important to see your role here.

The Solution

The solution they found is not a physical recuperation or changing your mind (even though that's what will happen) but a Spiritual solution. First the Spiritual condition, then the mental and physical will follow. The problem resides in the mind. In other words, we're not going to seek the solution from the problem. We're going to admit the problem and then ask for a solution from somewhere else.

The actions to access this Higher Power are the 12 steps. That's the whole basis of it to me. It says, *seemingly hopeless state of mind and body*. In that statement, it is not saying it is a hopeless state of mind and body because if it were, how could we have recovered? If it was a hopeless state of mind and body, there would be no solution. You would just have to hunker down and try to minimize the effects. But it says it's a *seemingly hopeless state*.

You now see that it is not a hopeless state, it just appeared to be, to us.

The First Addiction

I would say that the first addiction is the mind being addicted to the idea of being a self, (selfing) the sense of being a long-lasting, independent, separate entity. The expression of this addiction is a devotion to the thought system. Its result is an identification with the body.

No-thing, (a Higher Power) is seemingly forgotten as the body-thing is remembered. How is the body-thing constantly remembered? By being thought about. The thought system is rooted in its firm conviction that we are a body. The thoughts are used to suggest that we are the thinker or the thought about subject--object.

Self is remembered through time. When you are thought about in the past, you are remembered as a body, now. Thoughts of the future are being used to remember you as a body, now. The mental claiming of the thoughts, feelings and actions are being used to reinforce the idea of being the thinker, feeler and doer.

My thoughts, my feelings and my actions are being used to imply the seer, the doer and the actor. Conscious contact: Seeing, hearing, tasting, smelling and feeling, is being used to imply the one who is conscious. Thoughts are always about something and when something is thought about, that something is distorted.

The first addiction spawns all other addictions. All the other drives to escape were attempts to get relief from the first addiction. The dilemma is that the problem is identification as self. If the self attempts to escape from the self, that's just more self. As we say in AA, self cannot get out of self. Therefore the only way to get out of self is to realize you are not in self.

The alcoholic and/or addict has lost the ability to control their drinking and/or using. Unknowingly, the host has been taken over by a parasite (alcoholism). For all intents and purposes, you are being used to get its food.

You may not believe this, but there are plenty of examples in nature of how the parasite overrides the strongest instinct, self preservation of the host. There is a mushroom from the cordyceps family that has a unique way of overcoming it's handicap concerning reproduction. It has spores and it's in a stationary position where it can't deliver the spore where the spore is most likely to grow. It's degree of difficulty is extreme because it is basically relying on chance to succeed. What it does is the spore targets an ant and burrows into the ant, jacks into its brain and tells the ant where the mushroom wants to go. As soon as the ant arrives at the mushroom's destination, the spore kills the ant and then a mushroom grows out of the ants head. If we were the ant in this story, in self centeredness, we would have a whole narration about the trip of the spore after it took us over. We would be claiming every one of the spore's intentions and actions coming through us as our own intentions and actions.

Abstinence is Key

There is a hope that if I do enough, then somehow I will reach a stable state. It's like the Tibetan Buddhists' example of the hungry ghost, he has a very big belly but a very small mouth; no matter how much he eats, he can never get enough. That's active addiction. Abstinence is the key. If you don't have the first drink, the chain reaction of addiction won't start. If you have one, you're gonna have another. Maybe not that night, but pretty soon. It's the first drink that will get you drunk.

It's not about ever finding anything because it's never about the drug, it's about the addiction of self. That is what's causing all the other addictions such as eating, sex, gambling, shopping and everything else.

People are trying to get out of something that they are not in. That's why nothing works. If it worked, you would not have to keep applying it every freaking day, because it would work. It's like having a tool that works and then you put it away, you would honor that tool but you wouldn't have to pick it up again.

My view is that you've got to go to the **first addiction** if you want relief from the 3rd, 4th, 6th, and 9th addiction. All of these addictions are your mind trying to manage the irritability, restlessness and discontent of an unfulfilled first addiction, which is the addiction of becoming what you think you're not and unbecoming what you think you are, and becoming what you think you are, and unbecoming what you think you're not. Mental agitation begets agitation. It takes the body and uses it as an object and fixates on it. It expresses its fixation in time. By having a past and future it can go back to as the body, it can project itself and then worry about what's going to happen to it as a body. It's incessantly going over and over all of these mythical possibilities, not for any solution but to remember self.

What's not Happening

What people are calling fear, which runs through the fabric of our existence, is really mental anxiety. I like to call it--what's not happening. The mental anxiety is produced but it's not by the situation right in front of us, fear would be provoked if someone were threatening me right now. The emotion of fear would arise, my heart would quicken, the adrenaline would set in and I would 'take flight or fight'.

Obsession with Self

What's happening is an obsession with self, with this object-body in time. The mind and that activity is producing mental anxiety that actually mimics the physiological effects of fear. It's not fear, it's anxiety because there's no apparent threat now. Yet I could be reacting in a huge amount of anxiety right now because I'm not really responding to here, I'm reacting to there and then. This is the realm of the addiction of mind, of self. Self can only seem to appear in time.

You have no validation that you are a self right now except by looking at the body and calling it me. There's no way that you are the same person that you were when you were two years old. Everything about you has changed, it's always changing. That which isn't so can only appear to be so by being remembered in time. The idea that the same person spans babyhood, childhood, adolescenthood, adulthood, seniorhood, through all of those changes, that there would be one independent entity, is tenuous at best. No matter how much we change, all the changes are strung like pearls on a necklace used to infer a continuous, long-lasting, independant separate entity, me. This does not hold up under investigation.

It's called the obsession with self, the desire to become that image which can never be (at least for long) fulfilled, but continues in this hope that somehow, someday it's gonna work out (just not today). You need relief because it's unbearable. If you are all you think about all day, it will be so unbearable you would do almost anything to have it stop. And some of us have.

Uprooting The Root

Once you realize that the drinking and using are symptoms, then you start to see the root of the problem is that **you are** the problem, and once you start telling the truth about being the problem, there is another place that it can take you. **That place is when you thoroughly own what you are not, then what you are not, will become obvious.**

When the mental denial is pushing away all the things you don't want to be, you will be more of those things than ever, so we are not going with that mental denial; we are going with a very holistic, let's say Spiritual denial. To counteract the mental denial, we have to tell the truth about ourselves. **What our head would like to push away, let that land.**

We have to sit with the sense of what we've been trying to avoid for many, many years and to let it finally land.

You don't want that sense of unworthiness to arise, that feeling of, "You're never going to be enough," or "You're never going to be loved," **all these archaic beliefs that are like the catacomb of this conditional appearance.** You don't want to face up to that, therefore you are run by them every day. You're trying to move away from them, yet their influence grows larger as you try to move away. We are going to tell the truth to our innermost self. We are going to admit that-- "I'm an alcoholic."

I remember meeting this woman. She went to LA and met my old Tai Chi Master, and he told her, "Watch out for Paul because he's a user." That hurt the 'me' so much, but when I accepted that and let it land, and let it really, really be me, it's going to ultimately reveal that it's not me.

That's the radical freedom. You cannot get the radical freedom from pushing away things and acting as if you are not that. If you finally let it hit you and let it be as much as it wants to be you, it will reveal that it's not. That is the way of AA, to me.

Deep down there was something I was denying. It's like if you don't want to be a fraud, you will feel like one, thousands of times. If there's a strong desire that says, "I don't want to be the way that I am," you will feel that way, thousands of times.

See how the conditional mind works. It may strive to be in the moment, yet all of that striving is based on the insane idea that you could be out of a moment. Some are constantly trying to get out of self when all the while we could not possibly be one. We're in a bizarro world where in is out and out is in.

We're trying to get in what we can't be out of and trying to get out of what we can't be in.

When you step out of it, you can begin to see the building of that hallway of shit and fans. You can see what turns on the fans, you can see the shit as it aligns with it. When you step out of it, you can see the blueprint of the hallway of shit and fans and you'll see that what brings the shit and fans into possibility is you. If you're withheld, there is no hallway of shit and fans. If you're engaged, you're in the hallway of shit and fans.

In the *Big Book,* it says our daily reprieve is contingent upon the maintenance of our Spiritual condition. Let's say I take myself to be a body and a brain, this is what I am. A lot of things have not worked in my life, so let's say I get down to the last house on the block which is Spirituality. I'm now going to approach Spirituality as if I am a body. I'm going to become Spiritual. But this body is a thing. How is this thing going to become a no-thing? What kind of glue are you going to find that will stick no-thingness onto this thing? How are you going to absorb no-thingness in this conditional mind that's whole system is based on being a thing?

You cannot use that system to find out your own nature. For me, it's just recognizing that you are not what the system presents you to be and then your own nature will be revealed.

Pause

No-Thing

Mind is like space and empty sky. When a bird takes a shit, it doesn't land on the sky. A myriad of things appear in the sky, but do they stay long? How long do they stay? What lasting effects are left with all the passing phenomena? Does a firework display scar the sky? Do airline Captains call the tower to report a run-in with a large chunk of sky? Many things appear in the sky, but nothing affects the sky. Do bombs blow up the sky? You can have explosions in the sky but it doesn't cut the sky open. When it rains, the sky doesn't get wet. The sky is like what I call Mind. Mind allows all of this to appear but it never gets affected by what's appearing in it. I've never seen it, I've never seen what's seeing. It's nature is not of thing. Like Jesus said, "We are in this world, but not of it." This world is of things, but you are not of things. You are something else. I would say no-thing.

This, for me is the true solution of AA. The realization of what you're not. Through that realization, there is the finding out of what you are--a Spiritual condition. This is the true Spiritual condition. Not to be maintained as if you are something other than that, but to realize you are a Spiritual condition. That, to me, is the highest form of maintenance of a Spiritual condition, is to be a Spiritual condition. **By realizing what you are not, you will find out what you are.**

You will realize that you are what is looking, like Saint Francis of Assisi says, "What's looking, is what you are looking for." He doesn't say, 'who' is looking, he says 'what's' looking.

That you--looking for, is a who. We can never see the 'what,' for that is the seeing, that's why we can't see the what. But *what's looking is what you are looking for*. At the exact moment that you are looking for, that's what's looking. **But it's not you, it's what.** It comes to you. Really. It's like a Zen bitchslap. That's what it's like. NOTHING happens and that proves to be everything.

It doesn't mean that the expression or system of self-centeredness stops, it doesn't. Change, it will, but now the change will be directed by the Spirit, not the mental state. It's just that your interest and attention has been withdrawn from that dead preoccupation.

Editor's Note

The following pages are Paul's interpretation of, *The Twelve Steps of Alcoholics Anonymous.* Paul has not re-written the steps, but is sharing his experience, strength, and hope as he sees it.

If at any time you feel you are in need of psychological help, it is suggested that you reach out to a professional who can help you. There are some people in *Alcoholics Anonymous* who are in need of more than what the program offers, but who can still recover.

All of the Steps come directly from the *Big Book* of Alcoholics, they have not been changed or modified. Anytime you see the letters BB, it is in reference to the *Big Book* of *Alcoholics Anonymous.*

Thank you

Introduction

To me, the freedom doesn't come from the steps, the steps are just a portal for Grace to come in. It's the Grace, that *Power* of that Higher Power, that's what's initiating, fulfilling, filling up and completing any movement in my life. It's not something that I did, but through doing, it opened me up to a new direction.

Without Grace, the Twelve Steps would be hollow, in a way. They would be sound principles but they would be open to fundamentalism and a dogmatic view of it. It's the livingness and the release from alcoholism--that, to me, is what's valuable. That's the freedom. That's the message.

In the program, there's a lot of emphasis on doing and having, and in a sense, that is needed based on where people seem to be when they come into the program. There's an important observation at the beginning of AA that says you're going to act your way into good thinking instead of thinking your way into good acting. The 'where people seem to be,' changes quite a lot based on us staying on the operating table, not getting up and not playing doctor.

The song of recovery may start out as a 'forced march,' but more and more possibilities for an easier, softer way becomes available.

In the *Big Book* at the bottom of page 84, it states: *And we have ceased fighting anything or anyone, even alcohol. By this time, (around step 10 in the process) sanity will have returned. We will seldom be interested in liquor. If tempted, we recoil from it as from a hot flame. We react sanely and normally, and we will find that this has happened automatically. We will see that our new attitude toward liquor has been given us, without any thought or effort on our part. It just comes! That is the miracle of it. We are not fighting it, neither are we avoiding temptation. We feel as though we had been placed in a position of neutrality--safe and protected. We have not even sworn off. Instead, the problem has been removed. It does not exist for 'us'. Now that's a solution. We are not producing these effects, we are the expressing of them.*

We do not change, we are changed.

There was a priest at the beginning of AA's forming that said, *"Most people's experience of the program is a moving away from hell, not moving towards heaven."* In my experience there was a point where the flames of hell (if you don't do this, you're gonna drink) weren't enough.

I needed something else to inspire me to go in the right direction, not the fear of "What would happen if I drank?" but the desire to have a direct sense of the Source, of that Grace that had changed me.

Step One

**We admitted we were powerless over alcohol--that our
lives had become unmanageable.**
(First three chapters, BB)

When I first heard the statement of *powerlessness over alcohol
and our lives had become unmanageable,* at that time it seemed
like cause and effect. The cause of the unmanageability was
that I was drinking and I couldn't stop drinking. My belief,
when I came to *Alcoholics Anonymous* was if I could just stop
drinking, then my problems would cease. I was in for a rude
awakening.

I stopped drinking and the problems were even more glaring
because I wasn't dimming them down or covering them up
anymore. I prefer the statement in the *Big Book,* in *How It
Works* where it says there are three pertinent ideas we must be
convinced of and our experience before and after (meaning
before and after you get sober) will verify these three points.
The first one being: *We were alcoholics and could not manage
our own lives.* That fits better with me now because I don't
believe the powerlessness caused my unmanageability. I actually
believe the drive to manage my life came up with the solution
of alcohol for alcoholism, which produced tons of more
problems because **the real dilemma is that I'm not
managerial quality.**

I'm not meant to be running the show. I have to open up to some Power greater than myself, to offer me good orderly direction. Some people say that the first step is the only step that you can do perfectly. When I came into *Alcoholics Anonymous*, I had all the evidence I could ever need that *I'm powerless over alcohol and my life became unmanageable.* Prior to that statement in the *Big Book*, Dr. Silkworth talks about the twofold nature of the disease, a mental obsession and a physical allergy.

If you were allergic to strawberries and you ate strawberries, you would get hives, so no matter how many times you did not want to get hives, if you ate the strawberries you were going to get the hives. The solution then, is to deal with the obsession or the drive to eat strawberries because once you've eaten the strawberries, it's too late.

I admit that I am powerless and that my life had become unmanageable. You would think that when there's an admittance of powerlessness, you would experience powerlessness, but actually, it's the opposite. When you admit your powerlessness, you sense a new power. When you're managing and controlling, then you experience powerlessness. As soon as you attempt to manage and control, it's then that you start experiencing powerlessness. Those selfing experiences are frustrating because people aren't doing the things that you want them to do. It's not going your way, no matter how much you manage, it doesn't seem to pan out. The whole first step for me is an admittance that I am powerless over alcohol, and then I'm in a condition where I'm receiving power. We'll sense a new power flow in.

We admit that we are powerless over alcohol and our life has become unmanageable.

In hindsight, I found my drinking and using was an example that my managing was at the root of the unmanageability; the activity of the mental state we call 'playing God'. If the problem is the act of being identified as a self and the 'self' is what's playing God, how could that self stop playing God? Wouldn't that be called playing God?

I had to admit all the stuff that I had mentally been denying. As long as I was trying to make it unreal, it appeared to be as real, as real can be. When I finally let everything land on me, that is when I started to see it's unrealness.

First I have to finally accept what my mind's been denying for a long time, let it land and feel that uncomfortability. But then,---I'm not that. What my life was, was living in a mental, 'I'm not that' which made me seemingly 'be' that, every day. I was denying my inability to manage. I was denying my alcoholism and therefore, I lived alcoholically.

Now, instead of living in that mental denial, I go the other way and I admit to my innermost self that I'm an alcoholic, and at that point, the possibility of never living another day *as* one arises.

When you allow it to be exactly what it presents itself to be, which is 'you', you ultimately realize it's NOT you. That's the freedom from alcoholism. The freedom from alcoholism is freedom from self.

The Premise

The mental process I call, 'selfing' is constantly implying, assuming, presupposing, referring, and reinforcing an idea of what we are, and that is that we are a thing. I call it the activity of 'selfing', where a mental process is assuming this sense of being a long-lasting, independent, separate entity. You didn't have it when you were about a year old, you did not have a sense of being a separate 'you'. But then the mental process developed, (some say the sense of self appears as the brain's language center develops) it's then that the feeling of 'you' starts arising.

What you actually are is best to be found out by realizing what you're not.

Imagine for a moment that a hostile parasite takes you over. By its hostility, the host would be motivated to throw it off. So the parasite confronted with this dilemma devised a great strategy. In the mind, it presents itself as the host which neuters the possibility of the host ever being freed from the parasite; even when the host attempts to leave, it will attempt to leave as the parasite. So, is there any real leaving? No. For that parasite to continue to thrive, it would have to have a great strategy in which it convinced the host to not throw the parasite off. What does it do? It's my feeling that the parasite of alcoholism is jacked into that mental process that produces the sense of being "you" and it influences that "you" that the system produces. And now, that "you" that it produces, becomes an "alcoholic you."

"The root of the problem is obsession with self." (BB page 22-23)

I believe it's gone past that.

I don't believe it's obsession **with** self, I believe its identification **as** self. The obsession *with* self and all other obsessions that the selfing claims is being used to reinforce the identification **as** a self.

It's sort of like a horror movie where some woman really adores this one starlet and she starts wearing the same clothes as the starlet. She starts going to the same places as the starlet, and starts trying to date the same man as the starlet. And after that, that's not enough--she starts killing the men and soon enough she wants to kill the starlet and become the starlet. You might then say, "Wow, that's an extreme obsession," but I think that identification is *way, way* past that.

You take yourself to be what the mind is presenting you **as**. The mind is presupposing you as a certain 'self.' That's its basis. That basis demands relief from that basis, which is irritable, restless and discontent. You are going to want to get relief for that which you want to get relief from--but you're not going to get relief **from** it. You're going to get relief **as** it and **for** it, thus fueling the need for more relief--**reinforcing the idea of being the one that needs relief.**

To me, the real bondage of self, is through identification. If you take yourself to be the parasite, you can never entertain being free **from** it. It can only entertain being free **as** it. So, it goes through therapy and this and that in the socialization of it and tries to make it so it won't ruin the next relationship. It hopes to be okay at the next picnic that it goes to. The idea of success gets so low because you can't be free of it, because you're taking yourself to **be** it. There is no bondage to self, there isn't one. It's bondage **of** self, implying an activity.

That would be the greatest strategy of any parasitical movement--to convince the host that it is the host.

When we go to recovery meetings, a lot of people are sharing what it's like to be an alcoholic. They're sharing their feelings and thoughts and reactions to life.

So, you're sitting there for a few months and you're listening to this and you're probably in a very strong sense of terminal uniqueness because that's one of the qualities of the disease, is to feel like no one can understand you, no one thinks like you, no one feels like you, no one has done the heinous things that you have done. Yet you're sitting in a room, and people are seemingly sharing your thoughts, your feelings, and your actions that you too have done in life. You can only come to two conclusions. How did these people get *my* thoughts, *my* feelings and *my* behaviors? Or, they're not my feelings, they're not *my* thoughts, they're not *my* behaviors.

A normal person comes into a meeting and some of the things that we say, they would be aghast at, but all the people that have alcoholism can identify and they start laughing.

It's not who you are, it's what's taken you over. It's that dominant of a strain, of a parasitical movement, that you will take yourself to be that and you will have the same thoughts that any other alcoholic has, with similar feelings and similar reactions and still not see the impersonalness of it. One mental parasite, many, many hosts, all thinking they're unique. A great disguise--one, appearing in many.

For me, the first step was just a living statement of the problem. There are two facts in my life; before and after sobriety. One--I'm powerless over alcohol and drugs, two--I'm not managerial quality. So when I was using, I was in denial of these two facts and my life was the expression of that denial. When I got sober, those facts were still facts but now there was an admittance and acceptance of them. From that pivot, my entire life changed. In denial, life went one way. In acceptance, life had a chance to go another way.

While you are trying to get out of it, you're in it more than ever.

The mind moves in different ways and it has different strategies and yet most of them don't work. It's a failed system. That's why in the program of recovery, they say in the *Fear Inventory*, "Why are you in so much fear today?" and it doesn't let you answer because you'd probably tell a huge story about circumstances. NO, no, no, no !

Isn't it because self-reliance has failed us?

We have become reliant on a system of thought and interpretation called selfing. We have become so reliant on it that we take ourselves to **be** how it pictures us. When I did drugs, I never became the drug I was doing. I never crossed a line and became cocaine. What I am suggesting now is that 'me' is the product of selfing. I have taken myself to BE a foreign installment. It's using me for transportation, as an opportunity to express itself. It's a parasitical movement of mind, that's what alcoholism is. What the real addict could never reach from using, becoming the drug that they were using, in the mental addiction, the mental state has become identified with the drug of self. The mental state is starting at that point of being identified as the drug that it's addicted to--which is self, that a drug addict with a life long use could never reach. I loved cocaine, but I never thought I was coke, not once, not ever.

I'm not identified with *who* is in the room, I'm identified with *what* has taken them over because the same parasite that they are talking about as living under, I have lived under and I recognize it.

That's what is so beautiful about recovery. It allows people to come into a room, anywhere in the world and share what it is like to be an alcoholic and also, now, what it is like to be free from alcoholism. It's incredible.

Not Quite Step Two

They arise out of ourselves, and the alcoholic is an extreme example of self-will run riot. (page 62, BB)

There was a man in the beginning of *Alcoholics Anonymous* named Dr. Silkworth. He's the one that presented the idea that alcoholism was a disease. I once heard a very good definition of what disease means--it has three qualities: **It's progressive, it's chronic, it's life-threatening and alcoholism falls under those three categories:**

It's **progressive**: The consequences of it and the depth of its takeover will progress.

It's **chronic**: Basically, there's no break from it.

It's **life-threatening**: Alcoholism does not have an arm to reach for a drink, it doesn't have a vein to put a needle in. But it does have a demand and to answer that demand, it needs us for transportation, to express through. It likes fuel and the fuel is alcohol and drugs. If you give it its fuel, it gets stronger, it becomes all encompassing and quite unruly and you may find yourself in many life threatening situations.

Dr. Silkworth goes on to say that the disease is of the mind and body. The aspect of the mind is that it's based on an obsession. For me, the obsession was to get out of the discomfort I felt I was in. That was the imperative. But the thing is, 'it' cannot drink so it has to convince the host that it would be a great idea to have a drink. Even though the host may have had tons of experiences that that is not a great idea, the mental obsession brings you to a point that I like to call, *fuck it*. It may take a couple of days, it may happen very quickly, it may take years, but it starts setting up a story and that story usually leads the character 'you' to a point of *fuck it*. Once you hit *fuck it,* a voice is heard that sounds a lot like 'you' now rushes in with its solution, "Let's get loaded," or "Let's get high," or "Let's sleep with my best friend's girlfriend," and if there is compliance, there are consequences.

Let's say your mind has a tendency to be jealous and now you take a drink, that tendency to be jealous gets amplified. Before you were just having trouble in your head, now you're up on stalking charges, now you're breaking into your girlfriend's email. These are the types of things that happen, so as soon as it gets its fuel, it's too late. You're now basically on a run and you're not going to listen to any kind of yapping because you're not done.

The point is, you cannot deal with alcoholism after it's begun to flourish like that. You have to get it before it has the first drink. You have to have a change in mind concerning the insanity that precedes the first drink.

AA found that it has to be a Spiritual solution. Other people get sober and still they don't have any belief in a God, but to me, the program in and of itself is Spiritual. It doesn't need a God or any kind of deity because it's drenched in Spirit. **There is Grace in it.** They discovered that they have to deal with it at the obsession level because you won't get drunk unless you take the first drink. Before the first drink is where you want the immunity to be, not the twentieth one.

The alcoholic calls you after they drink, the recovered alcoholic calls you before they drink.

In alcoholism, you are totally dominated by a mental condition called self-centeredness. Everything is seen as how it pertains to you. We're seemingly blocked out from what we would call the sunlight of the Spirit. The mental condition obscures your Spiritual condition. That's the only way that it can thrive. It must precede the light (which it cannot do) to obscure it. If seen from light, the parasite would be seen as activity. It's our believing in the pointing that breathes imaginary life to the 'pointed at' now called the body.

The whole drive of the parasite is to keep you in the mental realm. The mental realm is all about 'you', somewhere else at some other time, what's not happening. Instead of seeing life is happening like when you were a kid, now it's seen as life is happening to you. It's a huge interpretation. Therefore there are many, many sleights that seem to be real and many, many disappointments that come out of this machination of an interpretation which demands relief. Relief that's not relieving is the Petri dish that addiction grows in. This is what you would call the bondage of self. Bondage **of** self, not bondage **to**. Bondage is of self. Bondage comes from self.

No self, no bondage. The freedom from bondage is freedom from self.

They found that the solution was not trying to deal with it on that level, but to provoke or to surrender to another realm which is what we call the Spiritual realm.

Let's say you have a deck of cards. The way that I was taught in society and how I grew up was if you get your circumstances right and you get your conditions right, it would translate into happiness. You get the girl, you get the job, this and that, go to college and that will translate into a sense of real well being. That, first of all, didn't work for me. Some say, "Okay, I'll make the body really good, I'll get really healthy and that will translate into me being really okay." Then there's the mental condition; if you look at your circumstances and situations, they can be overridden by a mental condition, just like that. You could have everything you want, everything could be perfect, and yet you're being driven crazy by your head. The mental condition overrides the circumstances. The mental condition overrides the physical condition. You can be healthy as an ox and yet be totally bummed out. Most people are trying to have the circumstances and maybe they're trying to get healthy but the mental condition keeps overriding the effects of the other two.

What they offer is a fourth card in the deck, which is the Spiritual condition. The Spiritual condition can override the mental condition. It can override the body condition, and it can override the circumstances and situational conditions. You can outshine circumstances and situations. This is the Ace in the deck. If you rely on the Spiritual condition, it will outshine the mental condition. It will allow you to be where you could never not be, which is here and now.

I can tell you, the joy of living is not in remembering. To be alive now, is the only place where life is. This is what the Spiritual condition is.

First, we admit that we are powerless over alcohol. We can't have a drink because if we do, the genie is out of the bottle and we're totally possessed.

I believe the active aspect of the disease today is the desire to manage or play God. That, to me, is a main aspect of the dilemma.

There is an identification as what's playing God. My experience is if you ever access God, it's not playing God--it is God. This is very different than when the mental process is playing God. It's very different to be under the guidance of God than under the guidance of what's playing God.

I admitted the first step and accepted the unmanageability that was caused by my managing. I spent two years in Delancey Street and when I left, I didn't like those people, I didn't like what they did, but I had to admit that my life looked better with them running it than it ever did with me running it. I came to the conclusion that I could turn my life over to a dog catcher and he or she would do a better job with it than me.

The real problem is playing God or managing. You can still be under the influence of alcoholism without having touched a drop for years. With alcoholism, the drinking and drug use is just a symptom of it. It's just a way of trying to manage what is totally unmanageable, which is, you've got full-blown alcoholism.

Your drive to manage is an expression of the root of the problem.

We have a statement in recovery that says, *Self can not get out of self.* You can't seek a solution from the problem. It will present many solutions but none of them will be a solution to the problem. There'll be solutions *from* the problem which just exacerbates the problem over and over and over again. The whole point is, if self cannot get out of self, and I am identified as self, then every time that I rely on me, I'm relying on the problem. There is no solution to that. So let's just say, maybe, just maybe--**I'm not that.**

If I am not Paul, what's going to happen? There will be a loss of attention and interest in all that reinforces the idea of being Paul. The interest and attention that was enslaving me today through its preoccupation with what's not happening, will now be enriching me.

It's just a shift of mind.

Habits

When you come into AA, you're not going to think yourself into right action, you're going to act yourself into right thinking.

Remembering the problem resides in the mind, you don't want the problem to have much say in your sobriety. Repeated actions are going to produce habits which are actions without thought.

In my case, I don't think about going to meetings, I think about which one I'm going to go to. Willingness may not always look willing. The habits will bridge the gaps in the willingness which will ensure your participation in the solution.

Step Two

We came to believe that a power greater than ourselves could restore us to sanity.
(Page 44, BB)

Lack of power, that was our dilemma. We had to find a power by which we could live, and it had to be a *Power greater than ourselves.* (*page 45, BB*)

The second step, to me, is an observational step. What *Alcoholics Anonymous* says is you do not have to believe in anything; all you need to do is be **willing** to believe. Be willing to come to believe. It says: *We came to believe that a power greater than ourselves could restore us to sanity.* I came into recovery and I started to do what they told me to do, and I got better. My observation was, "Hey, I've gotten restored to sanity, I haven't drank in eight weeks."

This step is talking about a very specific insanity, it's not saying insanity about this or that, it's saying the insanity that *precedes* the first drink. That's what we get restored to sanity about. We get restored to a sanity or a sound mind about that.

A lot of people think that it hasn't really worked because they are still insane. You can be insane about a lot of things, but you won't be insane about that first drink anymore. I came to believe that something greater than me was restoring me to sanity, because it was. Instead of being on the street, I got a room in a Residence Hotel. I got a job. I wasn't going to jail. My health was returning.

My solution to my problems before I got into *Alcoholics Anonymous* was to make new problems to distract me from the older problems. In other words, I didn't want to deal with that pile of stuff, so I made a new pile of stuff that I wouldn't want to deal with. After the first few months of being sober, I realized I had not created any new stuff so I found the courage to look back at the old stuff and started to tell the truth about the old stuff.

I started to get relief because now I was not relying on a failed system. I was relying on some sound principles that actually work; that can produce an incredible rearranging. Recovery is like the greatest recycler. You can throw a life in that you might have deemed to be totally worthless; (I didn't think I had been doing anything good for years) you can throw that in there and what you get back is a rejuvenated life with that life now being put to use in service to others. It's so beautiful in recovery because one day I need to hear the message and you need to carry the message; and on another day, I carry the message and you need to hear it. It's an incredible recycling system. A part of *Tradition Two* states: *"A loving God is expressing itself in our group conscience."* As an experience of a recovery meeting, the sum will add up to a lot more than the individual participants.

If you're a little bit open to it and willing, you can have some power greater than you influence your day and you will live as if the problem does not exist for you for that day. That's a powerful solution for that problem because that problem is pretty damned influential when you are under it. To have it not seem to be real, a day at a time, is an amazing miracle to me.

There is a common statement made in AA: ***"We're not people who have problems, we are the problem."***

That's where I see that the problem is identification because if we are the problem, how could there be any solution? In identification, we seem to be the problem. The solution is, we are not that self we are identified as, we are the solution.

We are identified, yet identification does not make it so. In truth, that which is false can only 'seem' to be true to what's true.

When it Stabilizes

This is a very high form of relief when the problem does not exist for you. How it stabilizes is when it doesn't exist **as** you. That's how it changed for me. While I was still identified, I got moments and sometimes days of relief where it looked like it didn't exist for me anymore, but it always seemed to come back.

Maybe the root of the problem is not obsession *with* self. Maybe the root of the problem is identification **as** a self.

Let's say you have a cold and you think you have the flu. You take a lot of flu medicine and you follow the directions religiously and you spend a lot of money on it. You're not gonna get relief from the cold because you've taken it to be the flu. Really get specific about the cause and then you will realize the diminishment of the effects. You will see that once you tell the truth about that and start entertaining, "Hey, I may not be that--then, the radical relief comes in. And, when the relief stabilizes, you'll see what made relief seemingly unavailable before. Then you will know the tree by its fruits. You will know you're onto something by the results. That's what happened with me.

I was in recovery for about 10 years and then I heard this message outside of recovery. It really hit me, and I entertained it. It became like an unspoken *yes* in my gut. When I went back to the *Alcoholics Anonymous* book and I saw statements like, "*Self, is what has defeated us,*" or "*Any life run on self-will, can hardly be a success,*" what that word self now represented was a foreign contagion, a mental parasite.

As soon as I saw self as 'other', a possibility heretofore unavailable, suddenly became available--that I can be free from it!

Up until this point, all wanting to be free was for a self, through a self and by a self. Now, Freedom **from** it became possible.

How I found I left the failed system was realizing I was not the center of the system, which is--self. I am not a long-lasting, independent, separate entity. **I am not a body**. Once that was entertained, then radical relief came in and that radical relief has stabilized, so I feel like I'm onto something. That's basically it.

I come out of a tribe and I have a drive to want to be of help. If anything can happen through these writings that would illuminate someone's view, that's the whole point of it. It's sort of like if you were in hell and someone brought you to a bus stop and that bus took you out of hell. Wouldn't you like to mimeograph that bus route and send it back into hell so people can get out? That's the point.

Faith

The loop of self got broken by making a decision first based on hope because I had no belief yet. I hadn't *come to believe*--but I took a chance, and the hope, very quickly, turned into belief--because it works!

It's not a false advertising campaign saying you will be okay later. No, it actually produced relief. I wasn't drinking. I wasn't getting arrested. I found a place to live without having to act like I liked someone in order to have a place to stay. I started making decisions based on hope that quickly turned into belief based on evidence. Life sometimes brought me misfortune but now I have the eyes to see the fortune in it. The process is now a vehicle of faith, which to me, is assurance that even though it may look like it's not gonna work out, it always works out. This is so beautiful. Faith has been shifted from a failed system--reliance on self, to trusting something infinite.

Everyone has faith. How faith manifests is based on the vehicle it is put in. Faith in a failed system of thought is going to produce anxiety--you're gonna be scared for no visible reason because you are going to be worried about what's not happening all day. The same faith put into centeredness, produces an ease and comfort in your own skin. You and I do not direct the faith. We are, as action figures, the expression of faith. Jesus was purported to have said, "As you believe, so it shall be done unto you." It's the exact same energy, it's just what it's put in to. This program shifts it from a failed system and puts it into a reliable system. Perhaps there is a better way. Trust in something infinite rather than finite self.

When I realized "I'm not that," I immediately entertained I could be free from it. As long as the identification with self was in place, I could only entertain freedom for that. Now, that relief has stabilized, and it appears as travelling lighter.

Almost Step Three

On the other hand--and strange as this may seem to those who do not understand--once a psychic change has occurred, the very same person who seemed doomed, who had so many problems he despaired of ever solving them, suddenly finds himself easily able to control his desire for alcohol, the only effort necessary being that required to follow a few simple rules. Page xxix--Big Book.

For a long, long time there was no solution to alcoholism; winos were talked about in the *Psalms* of the Old Testament. Here's someone who can't stop drinking, who's creating huge consequences in his life. It's affecting everyone in a nasty way around them and suddenly that someone makes a complete about face.

There is an important phrase in chapter five, in *How it Works*, that says: "Self-knowledge avails us nothing." Now that sounds wild because a lot of value is put on knowledge in this world, but here he's saying self-knowledge will avail you nothing. What is knowledge and self knowledge? Let's say I'm receiving knowledge about my condition, I'm learning about alcoholism. This knowledge can be very valuable, but if I'm identified as the parasite, that knowledge will be claimed by the problem and will not lead to relief of the problem. I'm taking myself to be the parasite, called self. When the knowledge about self is offered to me, what's receiving it is a mind *in* self. That knowledge about self will not lead me to freedom *from* self because the self is claiming it. It's saying, "I'm the one who's just learned about me." This is one of the fundamental traps of identification *as* self. When you are identified *as* self, you'll never know it, until Grace shows up and/or you hear it from the outside.

*When the identification is in place, what is not you, is taken to *be* you. There's no question about it. You may question if you're good or bad, or if you're not enough, but you're not going to question the basic fundamentals of being *you*. The mind is not going to go there.

In that situation, the main movement of selfing is claiming; it takes advantage of anything it comes in contact with. In other words, it has your life. That's how it's living. It needs a life to live through, it cannot live in and of itself because it doesn't have an existence. It exists on the host.

If that psychic condition of being identified as self is in place, no matter how much you learn about you, it's not going to lead to freedom *from* you. It's not going to produce its true value unless it leads to the freedom *from* self.*

It's like the professor of holes. He knows all about holes, but he keeps falling in the holes. So what's the point of that knowledge? This whole idea of *self-knowledge availed us nothing,* is a very big statement to me because the movement of selfing (which is what we are identified with) is to claim or to take advantage of, therefore neutering the value of the knowledge.

A famous Zen master, Dogen, says to study Buddhism is to study the self, to study the self is to forget the self. So instead of self knowledge, if there is knowledge of self it will lead to the forgetting of self because you will see that it is **not** you. When things are not about you, you usually lose interest in them.

It's Presented As 'My'

Take this book that you're reading as an example. The book is seemingly an object in and of itself. If you want to change that, it can become my book. What does the my do? When the book is affixed with the my, the book points to the owner of the book. This is what selfing does. This is how it gets a reflection of itself all day. Instead of a body, it's my body.

Whose body is it? My body.
Who is that my?
What is that my inferring?
What is that my pointing to? It's pointing to the self thought.
They are my thoughts.
Who is that my?

Do you ever see that my, or is it inferred by the claiming of all the activities of the body and the brain? **It's like a finger pointing to a phantom, yet because it's always being pointed at, it takes itself to be so.**

The difference between a thought and my thought is unbelievable. A thought has the nature of coming and going, you don't know where it came from and you don't know where it goes. It appears on the screen of consciousness and there's an awareness of it. What happens if a thought comes in my head? As soon as that thought is claimed to be **mine**, the system of thought and interpretation called selfing now injects meaning into that thought. The thought is not bringing you a new meaning about something outside of you, it's a container and it gets injected with additional meaning that you have about you, into that thought. Then, the thought opens up by awareness and now you believe that the thought is bringing you all this information when the information was downloaded from a previous thought, the thought of being *you*. This is the activity of the bondage of self. If I hold a thought to be a thought, it's so much lighter than when it becomes my thought.

Let's say there are 70,000 thoughts a day. Let's say each one of those thoughts weighs an ounce and let's say in your day, you're aware of 3,000 thoughts. Each one of those thoughts weighs an ounce, so every day that you are attending to the thoughts, you're traveling with 3,000 ounces of weight. You've been traveling like this for quite a while so you don't even notice it. It's like having a backpack on that you don't even know that you have on. You're used to it. You go through your day, you go through your relationships and it seems to be, "Hey I'm just traveling the way everyone else is traveling." Now, let's change the thought into my thought.

Let's say on a blackboard you put the word 'relationship', you put the word 'health,' you put the word 'money,'--now look at it. Now, let's change it dramatically--add the word my. My money, my health, my relationships. Now, stand and hold both of those. Hold it as relationships, health, and money--now hold it as my relationship, my health, and my money. What's the difference? Huge difference. There's a weight to it. You don't see it, but it is much heavier.

That's what people are traveling under. Instead of 3,000 ounces, they're traveling with 3,000 pounds and I'm telling you, when you're traveling with 3,000 pounds, there's going to be something in you that wants relief. It's going to become the main imperative. You're going to be seeking for something every day because you're carrying around a lot of weight; a lot of freaking weight. You can't put it down because it's *yours*, there's been a claiming of it. When you try to put it down, it adds more to the weight.

You cannot have freedom from a thought system as a thought. The you that's constantly being thought about, is a thought. It's like when you're at a park and you're looking at 30 kids. Where does your attention go? To the one that's yours, yes? My attention is going to rest on the one kid that I call mine.

That's exactly what happens with thoughts. Thoughts keep showing up and showing up but if they're held as my thoughts, I'm telling you, your interest and attention is going to follow that thought. When your interest and attention goes with a thought, it goes into that mental realm, and you will seem not to be here; you're in a mental here that is chock full of there and then. If you are not here, you're not going to be satisfied. No matter how much you have, no matter how much you've done, no matter how much you're thinking you're going to do, you're inherently not going to be satisfied here. You can tell that you're not satisfied because you will be seeking, yes? Seeking, seeking, seeking.

This is what the my does. It plays God. This is the main thing. This is what my is. My is the expression of that which is playing God.

A thought is a thought until it's mine, then it has a function to imply the thinker. This is the obsession with self. This is how it constantly gets reflection with everything that it comes in contact with. It emphasizes self, through the my. Everything it comes in contact with is claimed and used as a mirror to reflect *you* the doer, *you* the haver, *you* the long-lasting, independent, separate entity. That's the addiction of selfing.

Alcoholism is like a parasite that affixes on another parasite called self-centeredness. Alcoholism acts as an amplifier of self-centeredness. Certain qualities of self-centeredness will be become exaggerated in expression, through alcoholism.

What I'm saying here is maybe, just maybe, you are not that. If you are not that, what gets freed is the interest and attention. Interest and attention is like a bloodhound, it's going to go to whatever you believe to be you. If you think you're an idea, if you think you're an image, if you think you're the body,--that interest and attention is going to keep going to you, your body condition, keep going to your mental condition or going to your emotional condition. You'll want to get relief from it but you can't call it off. But **if you are not that**, the owner of the body, if you are **not** the thinker of the thoughts, if you are **not** the doer of the action, then you can have relief from the actions, relief from the thoughts.

If my eyes are open, I'm going to see whatever goes by. Am I the one that's seeing that? Or is that idea an afterthought to the seeing? The seeing is first. Conscious contact is the activity of what I am.

Consciousness in contact, is feeling, seeing, tasting, smelling, and hearing thoughts,--that, is conscious contact.

I'm talking about freedom from the bondage of self. When you are bonded to that **me** as being *you*, you forget the "I," you forget what you are, and you seemingly forget the Spirit. Now you're looking for it out there, when you *are* that which you are looking for.

You can spend years or lifetimes looking for it. You're never going to find what you are, because *you are it*. But you are not it as it's presented by the mind, you are it as it's demonstrated by consciousness, by conscious contact. You **are** what is seeing, but you will never see it. You **are** what's hearing, but you will never hear it. You **are** what's feeling, but you will never feel it. That's the beauty of it.

You are so it that you will never have an experience of it. You are so it, that there's no way that you can get outside of it to have an experience of it.

Step Three

Made a decision to turn our will and our lives over to the care of God as we understood Him.
(Page 63, BB)

Paul: The third step is the main principle of the program. Obviously a decision is not the act itself, it's just making a decision that you are willing to do it. The act of doing that is in steps 4 through 9, that's the completion of the decision to turn your life over as it says in *How it Works*, on page 60-62 in the *Big Book*.

BB: *Being convinced, we were now at step 3, which is that we decided to turn our will and our life over to God as we understood Him. Just what do we mean by that, and just what do we do? The first requirement is that we be convinced that any life run on self-will can hardly be a success.*

Paul: The definition of 'convinced' means to believe/know with certainty. Only by observing your past history will you come to that conclusion. You'll be very, very clear that you are not managerial quality.

B.B. *On that basis we are almost always in collision with something or somebody, even though our motives are good. Most people try to live by self-propulsion. Each person is like an actor who wants to run the whole show; is forever trying to arrange the lights, the ballet, the scenery and the rest of the players in his own way. If his arrangements would only stay put, if only people* *would do as he wished, the show would be great. Everybody, including himself, would be pleased. Life would be wonderful. In trying to make these arrangements, our actor may sometimes be quite virtuous. He may be kind, considerate, patient, generous; even modest and self-sacrificing. On the other hand, he may be mean, egotistical, selfish and dishonest. But as with most humans, he is more likely to have varied traits.*

Paul: In this aspect, we usually take the bad aspects of character to be self-will, but in this case, even the good aspects may still be vested in selfing.

BB: *What usually happens? The show doesn't come off very well. He begins to think life doesn't treat him right. He decides to exert himself more. He becomes, on the next occasion, still more demanding or gracious, as the case may be. Still the play does not suit him. Admitting he may be somewhat at fault, he is sure that other people are more to blame. He becomes angry, indignant, self-pitying. What is his basic trouble? Is he not really a self-seeker even when trying to be kind?*

BB: *Is he not a victim of the delusion that he can wrest satisfaction and happiness out of this world if he only manages well?*

Paul: This is one of the main delusions of alcoholism, right here. No matter how much evidence life shows you that you are not managerial quality, that urge to keep managing is very, very strong. You just think if only I did it better it will work. A lot of alcoholics that I know, they are not into changing themselves, they are into changing everything else around them. The last place that they look for the problem is themselves. They think they have a problem but they never realize, (they do finally), that they are the problem. When I was out there using, it was you that was driving me crazy. It was the police, it was my girlfriend, it was the drug dealer. I never looked at my role in things.

The whole point of recovery is to turn the light off of everyone else and everything else and to **let it shine on you.** That's where the solution lies.

BB: *Is it not evident to all the rest of the players that these are the things he wants? And do not his actions make each of them wish to retaliate, snatching all they can get out of the show? Is he not, even in his best moments, a producer of confusion rather than harmony? Our actor is self-centered--egocentric, as people like to call it nowadays. He is like the retired business man who lolls in the Florida sunshine in the winter complaining of the sad state of the nation; the minister who sighs over the sins of the twentieth century; politicians and reformers who are sure all would be Utopia if the rest of the world would only behave; the outlaw safecracker who thinks society has wronged him; and the alcoholic who has lost all and is locked up. Whatever our protestations, are not most of us concerned with ourselves,our resentments, or our self-pity? Selfishness self-centeredness! That, we think, is the root of our troubles. Driven by a hundred forms of fear, self-delusion, self-seeking, and self-pity, we step on the toes of our fellows and they retaliate.*

Paul: Take note on the word self that precedes every one of those statements. If you look in the dictionary at the word Spirit, there will be one definition but if you look up the word self, there will be a hyphen and one hundred descriptive adjectives that follow--self-satisfaction, self-hatred, self-love, self-abuse, etc.

BB: *Sometimes they hurt us, seemingly without provocation, but we invariably find that at some time in the past we have made decisions based on self which later placed us in a position to be hurt.*

Paul: I have a simple example of that. Let's say that I'm on a prison farm and the guy who's on the horse does not like me. So, during the day when I'm out doing some chores at the farm, this guy rides up to me and spits on me. I get really pissed off, I say, "Jesus Christ, I haven't done anything to deserve this." But if I looked at my behavior, I must have done something to end up in that prison farm. This is the whole point of investigation, is to try to take it back to where you had a role in things instead of looking at everyone else's role.

BB: *So our troubles, we think, are basically of our own making. They arise out of ourselves, and the alcoholic is an extreme example of self-will run riot, though he usually doesn't think so. Above everything, we must be rid of this selfishness. We must, or it will kill us! God makes that possible.*

Paul: So, our troubles are basically of our own making, but how are they being made? How are they constantly reinvigorated? Let's say I have 30 problems in a month, there's only been one 'me' who had them all. What role does the 'me' play in all the problems? When I looked over my relationships with women, most of them did not work. I looked at 18 of them, and I could come up with only one constant in all of those relationships and that was **me**. I didn't have the extreme bad luck to have run into 18 crazy women, I brought some of the craziness with me. Our view is so extremely off of us and on to others, situations and circumstances and it's causing a real sense of blindness to our true role in things.

BB: *And there often seems no way of entirely getting rid of self without His aid.*

Paul: How can you get rid of self, as self? If I go and study self for about two years, you could see that as an obsession with self. How is self, ever going to get out of self? The 'experience' of being out of self stabilizes when you see you were never in self.

BB: *Many of us had moral and philosophical convictions galore, but we could not live up to them even though we would have liked to. Neither could we reduce our self-centeredness much by wishing or trying on our own power. We had to have God's help.*

Playing God, The Unspoken Step

Paul: This is a very, very important part of the book.
BB: *This is the how and the why of it. **First of all, we had to quit playing God.** It didn't work. Next, we decided that hereafter in this drama of life, God was going to be our Director. He is the Principal; we are His agents.*

Paul: The unspoken step is quit playing God, which is gonna be very hard to do if you are identified as that which is playing God. Again you get stuck in that paradox of that which is playing god, playing god about playing god. **Because you're identified AS playing God.** How the hell are you gonna get out of that? You can only try getting out of that AS that while identified. This is the way it works. This is why I humbly believe the root of the problem is the identification as that which is playing God (selfing--the thought system) We're seemingly stuck, and any attempts to get out make it more stuck. But only seemingly so, because we are not that which is playing God. **I don't see any other diagnosis that could possibly work other than seeing that you are identified with that which is playing God.** If you see that you are not that which is playing God, that is how YOU can stop playing God, by realizing that you were never that which is playing god. That's God.

This is the unspoken step. If you read the way it's set up, you'll see its importance. The third step, is the keystone to the archway to freedom. In other words, all the other steps rest on the third step. For me, the identification as self is the epitome of playing God. It's like when you wake up in the morning and your head tells you how the day is going to be before you even get up, you actually believe it. What is that, but playing God? What is it that when it tells you how you are, how you were, how you are going to be, how they are, how they were or how they are going to be? There's a belief there in that. What is that but playing God?

In my experience of life, if you look at it like a card game and you're being dealt a hand and each moment is a different card, I noticed that you are not going to get the 4pm card at 8am, you are going to get the 8 a.m. card. But what happens when the mind is playing God? Even before it gets the 8 a.m. card, it has come to a conclusion about how all the cards are going to look that day. It totally plays God with life. You are not even available to find out because you, in a sense, know it's going to suck, you know it's going to go this way or that. That's like neutering life. It takes all the joy out of it. "I know it's going to suck today." How do you know it's going to suck, you haven't even shown up yet? This is the state of mind in selfing, the sense of being so sure when you actually have no idea.

You get a false security by this mental knowing, yet this knowing fosters an attitude of contempt prior to investigation. In Zen, they recognize one of the highest forms of mind as 'I don't know.' In the state of 'I don't know,' what occurs? You'll find out.

This is a much more convincing way of receiving knowledge--by finding out, than to try to believe you preemptively know something. That whole drive to know, for me, is like a way of neutering what's going on. If I know it from where I'm looking at it from, I'm never going to find out about it. If I think I know my girlfriend, I'm never open to finding out about her. If I think I know how the day is going to go, I'm not open to finding out how it's going to go. If I know who I am, I'm never going to find out what I am. It's the biggest deterrent to living--this preemptive knowledge. That's the act of playing God. For me, this is the unspoken step of the entire program. That's why it says first, *quit playing God* and then next, *God will be the principal and we will be his agents.*

BB: *He is the Father, and we are His children. Most good ideas are simple, and this concept was the keystone of the new and triumphant arch through which we passed to freedom when we sincerely took such a position.*

Paul: The position, which is that this power (if you wanna call it God, who cares what name you give it) now has been sincerely opened up to. It's usually because your ass got totally kicked, but now you have a sincerity. What's gonna happen to you?

BB: *all sorts of remarkable things followed.*

Paul: If we had a number of alcoholics, and we had them come up here to share just a couple of the remarkable things that have happened after they took this third step, this thing would go on like a marathon. There would be an unending stream of examples of the wonderful things that happened when this mind with alcoholism took this position of surrendering to a power greater than itself.

Service

BB: *We had a new Employer. Being all powerful, He provided what we needed, if we kept close to Him and performed His work well.*

Paul: Here, the whole aspect of future worry is taken care of in one fell swoop because He is going to provide what we need when requirements are met. The first one is, *if we keep close to Him.* For me, you cannot be far away from everywhere, if God is everywhere, then it's there right where you are because no matter where you are, you can't escape everywhereness. So, that first requirement is already kept. Second, *to perform His work well*. This aspect of performing His work well comes under the category of service which is one of the main tenets of the whole program. You are willing to give away what was freely given to you.

The program is represented by the symbol of a triangle which is--one side recovery, one side unity, and one side service.

Service is the tried-and-true practice of getting out of one's self. When you get out of one's self, what happens? You feel available. That availability gives a sense of being spacious, of presence, and through the presence you get to see how shut down you were. The solution allows you to know the problem. It's so incredible. It allows you to see how claustrophobic you were just before you did the service. Usually, in that spaciousness, what happens? The mind senses a presence of what we call the Higher Power. This is the beauty of it. By doing service, you will have a free sample of where you could live from.

BB: *Established on such a footing,..*
Paul: Let's say you've sincerely taken this position, now you are getting stabilized. In other words, you're living from that point of surrender.

BB: *..we became less and less interested in ourselves, our little plans and designs.*

Paul: I love that he uses the word little because when you're obsessed with self, everything seems really big.

BB: *More and more we became interested in seeing what we could contribute to life.*

Paul: If you 'try' to become more interested in what you contribute to life, that's actually being more interested in 'you.' Self can't get out of self. But now, the selfing is being affected by the solution and these are some of the results. It's diminishing the preoccupation of the mental obsession and what happens is you become aware of being conscious now.

BB: *As we felt new power flow in,..*

Paul: This is one of the most powerful things because we've been living on fumes. Selfing has no power. It plays God because it isn't God. It's doesn't have any God juice, it's using our God juice basically to play with. That's what it does because we are identified with it. We've unwillingly given over our God juice, in a sense, to this parasite and it's making a mental world for us to inhabit.

BB: *...as we enjoyed peace of mind,..*

Paul: If your head is constructed and beholden to time, even if peace of mind broke, how much would you enjoy it? Wouldn't your mind think, "Hey, it may not be here tomorrow." How can you enjoy the peace of mind if you are invested in time? Peace of mind is from timelessness, it's not a quality of time. If you have peace in time, it's gonna provoke anxiety because you're gonna be afraid that you will lose it. If you realize it's of timelessness, you realize there are no restrictions to your entertaining it, then there is an ability to relax in the peace. You can't relax into timelessness from self, because self is constructed of time.

The value in the thought system is past and future, it has very little value--now. Self could care less about this moment, it's concerned about where it is leading to and where it came from, which is that thought system called selfing or self-centeredness. That thought system presents you as a body, that's how it thinks of you. If you think about you in the past, how are you seen? You're seen as a body. You couldn't go back to the past without the identification as a body. You would realize there is nothing there. It's only when you appear in it, that the realm seems real. Doesn't it? It's when you picture yourself three years ago, it's then that the mind gravitates towards thinking about that, but if there was not a body to place there, your attention would never leave this moment.

Selfing, is playing God. It takes you as the fixation of the mind and places you somewhere else at some other time and then thinks about it. Your attention and interest gets glued to those thoughts and you basically vacate the here and now to seemingly be there and then.

I would say that is the root of our dilemma and yet the thought system will never point that out. To enjoy peace of mind, you have to be here to enjoy it and you can't fully be here as a thought of mind.

You, are just a conjuring up of past. The way I feel right now is just memory, it's just a production of mind. The aliveness gets deadened and the story of you gets stretched into time. All that interest that could provoke such a value in being alive is now attending to a story of you. You are the only person who is probably interested in it.

If people come to me and start telling me what's driving them crazy and it isn't happening now, I can't see it. I have total immunity to that. While the thoughts are driving them crazy, the same thought system that I have immunity to when it's seen as theirs, if I call it mine, it will drive me crazy. It's not the thoughts that have power, it's the 'my', it's the identification as the mind. It's the thought of being the thinker that gives the thoughts the juice they have. Would you blame the radio for the music playing through it ?

BB: *..as we discovered we could face life successfully,*
Paul: I always tell this story because it has been my Petri dish of learning how to face life successfully. My idea was that I didn't want to get rejected or be bad at anything, so my solution was not to try much. I wouldn't take any chances. In AA they say you've got to be willing to save your ass instead of your face but when I came in here I thought my face was my ass. I thought this mental image of me was my ass. That's what I was busily trying to save while I was losing my ass. My face can be lost and I'm quite happy about it, but I do need to save my ass. One of the first times I experienced this was the first AA dance I ever went to. Whoever is reading this right now will know what I mean when I say my first AA dance was my last. I was at the dance and I may have been about 6 months sober. I was on the men's side of the auditorium and the women were on the other side. I must have drank about 16 carbonated

waters because I didn't have beer anymore as a buffer, so I was just drinking anything I could. Nothing was happening. The music was on, the disco ball was going, but no one was asking anyone to dance. On the men's side, I became the scout and they sent me over to ask a woman to dance. There was a girl from afar that I thought I'd like and I wanted to meet her. It was sort of like no man's land. I crossed no man's land, totally obsessed with myself. I got over to the other side and I asked the girl to dance and she said no, which was the thing that I had been avoiding my whole life--that idea of being rejected. If anyone was going to reject me, I was going to reject myself first, and here was this girl. Instead of my mind rising up and saying, "Oh, I didn't really want to dance with her," I did want to dance with her; instead of trying to rationalize it away, I took the rejection and turned around. At that point, the space between the men and the women turned into a minefield and the disco ball turned into a spotlight. I walked across the minefield like an Indian with no scalp. The thing that I had been afraid of the most, I was feeling--which was rejection. At that moment, I realized that it didn't have the power to kill me because I was surviving it.

That was one of the first big experiences where I could face life successfully and I started to get the balls to ask for what I wanted, to go for what I wanted. I was willing to take the answer no. I learned how to face life successfully in *Alcoholics Anonymous*.

BB: *..as we became conscious of His presence,..*

Paul: *..as we became conscious of His presence,..* this to me, is one of the major gifts. If you're totally conscious of your presence all day, which is obsession with self, there's no way you're going to be conscious of Its presence. In other words, if you are going to have a real strong sense of Spirit's presence, there's gotta be a real strong sense of your own absence. Like Saint Francis of Assisi said, "It is in dying to **self** that **we are born** to eternal life." There are many, many Spiritual traditions that talk about the death of self or in losing self interest is how you gain interest in the sense of Spirit. When I'm present as a mental appearance, Spirit or reality is seemingly absent. When I'm not obsessed as this mental appearance, then the Spiritual presence is obvious. That's what happened. I became conscious of the presence of Spirit, which I believe is my own presence, as I lost interest in the mental process called selfing. It's only because I started losing interest in the mental process of selfing.

That's what this thing does, it produces a fake appearance, it's totally consumed in you and you become the presence in life and what's truly present seems to be absent and now you're looking for it all day.

When I lose interest in this idea of self then what's always available and has always been available becomes available. Not to me, but **as** me.

Centeredness

BB: *..we began to lose our fear of today, tomorrow or the hereafter.*

Paul: If we begin to lose our fear, that means there was a point where we had the fear. If we have the ability to outgrow something, we must have grown into it. For me, that's what happened. There was a growing into this identification as self, a growing into a reliance on the system of thought interpretation and self-centeredness which implies that you can grow out. Through the steps of AA, I started to outgrow that system and opened up to a different modality of mind. I would call that centeredness, not self-centeredness.

If that centeredness is everywhere, at all times, then the ability to feel centered is always available at all times. Self-centeredness is always based on mental circumstances and situations. Those mental circumstances will override what's actually happening.

But centeredness--it's always available at all times. The difference in living is huge. To me, I would call it traveling lighter. When the basis of your interest and attention is centered, then you **travel lighter.** When it's self-centered, you travel heavy, and if you're traveling heavy, there will be a demand for relief and the system itself will give you a solution, which is inherently part of the problem.

BB: *..we were reborn.*
Paul: This happened before step 3. I had already given up hope for quite a while regarding anything changing. I was just hunkered down in that lifestyle of trying to stay as loaded as I could until one of the three doors that you're usually parked in front of, opened--that being an institution, jail, or death.

Surrendered

The day I got sober, I was sitting in a trailer. A vertical insertion of 'something' or 'nothing' as I like to call it caused the stream of the conditional mind to stop and what came along with that was surrender.

I realized from my own experience what surrender means to me. For me it was delivered by Grace. Before this, you would think I would have surrendered after I got run over twice in one night or after I got shot at or overdosed but none of those things brought about a surrender. Surrender was given to me. It was downloaded. I had nothing to do with it, nor did circumstances and situations. That is what occurred, something that I call surrender occurred that day and from that day on, I could entertain surrender.

Entertaining surrender can lead to surrendered. Instead of being an act, it is now a state. Surrendered.

In my experience in AA, when the selfing is playing God, it's the sense of self that is claiming to be turning one's will and life over to the care of a Higher Power. In this deal, the self is always the Higher Power so when the self decides something is too important to turn over to God, it will take it back implying that it's the bigger God in the business.

A common experience I've seen is that people feel that they have surrendered but they take it back and then they surrender again--but they take it back. My view of that is sort of like a bully on the playground that gives a bag of candy to a little kid and says, "You keep this for me," and anytime he wants it, he just grabs it away. He does it because he's a bigger kid. That's the state of mind that has that experience as a continual thing. To surrender and take it back, means you must be the bigger God in that deal than the God that you have surrendered to.

That's not my experience anymore, once I started to entertain the idea of surrender, it actually turned into surrendered. Surrendered became a stabilized state where there isn't any giving it over and then taking it back anymore. That little circus act is over.

There's a state of surrendered which I think is available through the program of AA, it may not be entertained often but it is available. I know I never could have provoked the surrender, I mean I would have if I could have. I knew I was hell-bent for destruction but I couldn't seem to stop and surrender. Once again, it had to be given to me. First I had the experience of surrender and then I could entertain it. That's how the program has seemed to work for me. Just like when you entertain that you are not this long-lasting, independent, separate entity, this image of a body that the mind is obsessed over--then you can entertain being free from all of that obsession. Hey, you may want to look at this from page 60, in the BB:

There is a statement in AA that describes it: The first requirement is that we be convinced that any life run on self-will can hardly be a success. On that basis we are almost always in collision with something or somebody, even though our motives are good. Most people try to live by self-propulsion. Each person is like an actor who wants to run the whole show; is forever trying to arrange the lights, the ballet, the scenery and the rest of the players in his own way. His arrangements would only stay put, if only people would do as he wished, the show would be great. Everybody, including himself, would be pleased. Life would be wonderful. In trying to make these arrangements, our actor may sometimes be quite virtuous. He may be kind, considerate, patient, generous; even modest and self-sacrificing. On the other hand, he may be mean, egotistical, selfish and dishonest. But as with most humans, he is more likely to have varied traits.

What usually happens? The show doesn't come off very well. He begins to think life doesn't treat him right. He decides to exert himself more. He becomes, on the next occasion, still more demanding or gracious, as the case may be. Still the play does not suit him. Admitting he may be somewhat at fault, he is sure that other people are more to blame. He becomes angry, indignant, self-pitying. What is his basic trouble? Is he not really a self-seeker even when trying to be kind? Is he not a victim of the delusion that he can wrest satisfaction and happiness out of this world if he only manages well?

Closer to Step Four

*But it is clear that we made our own misery.
(page 133, BB)*

BB: *A business which takes no regular inventory usually goes broke. Taking a commercial inventory is a fact-finding and a fact-facing process. It is an effort to discover the truth about the stock-in-trade. One object is to disclose damaged or unsalable goods, to get rid of them promptly and without regret. (Page 64, BB)*

Paul: You're never gonna be able to get rid of anything if there is a sense that it is yours. This is the entire identification of self, that act of claiming. There is no way you can walk away from something without looking back, if you think it was yours. That's the radical freedom. The radical freedom is that it is not of you. When the sirens of Ulysses start calling, you don't look back because it has nothing to do with you, it's just been a parasitical movement of mind that you have been relieved of.

BB: *If the owner of the business is to be successful, he cannot fool himself about values.*

Paul: As an example: Let's say I have a clothes store. It's in a nice location in a mall and I do pretty good. I'm identified as the store owner and I feel pride in it. I take a gamble and I invest in 800 pairs of Elephant Bell Jeans; I'm thinking they're going to make a big comeback. I put them in stock in the back and you know what? No one is buying these jeans. I even give them to my girlfriend and when I'm not there, she returns them. No one's wanting these jeans.

I'm under a lot of pressure. Creditors are calling. I'm losing interest, people are coming in and stealing stuff, I'm not sweeping up. The condition of the store is going down. It seems to be like a failed system of business.

One day, someone walks in and says, "Hey listen, I'm really interested in taking over this store, I'll buy the store from you." I say "Gladly, where do I sign?" I want to get out from underneath this thing. I sign the papers and I'm ready to leave but the guy says "No, no, no, I want you to stay on and manage this place. You can work the place, but I'm the owner, alright?" I'm sitting there and the phone rings, I pick it up right away and a guy on the other side says "Is this the owner?" I say "No," and hand the phone to the new owner. That night, I go home, I talk to my girlfriend honestly about the troubles with the store because they're not mine anymore.

It's not mine anymore. It seems like everything shifted from being the owner of the store to not being the owner of the store. This is the nugget of the third step. You turn your will and your life, (the store) over to the care of something greater than you. To the new employer or the new owner, this is what shifts all the perceptions of the circumstances that you are in. What was deemed to be worthy of worry gets dismissed. That's how it happens, just by changing the sense of ownership. For me, this is the entire spirit of the 4th step.

Obsession With Self

I'm going to use a balloon to represent 'me' in this example:

The balloon has obsession with self and it's idea of success is to not be popped. That's the only thing it cares about. It doesn't care if it's used in a parade, it just doesn't want to get popped. The way it gauges how it's doing in this endeavor is by the thickness or thinness of its skin.

The balloon has alcoholism which is obsession with self, and that obsession with self is represented by air in this example. The more the balloon is obsessed with itself, the more air comes into it. Let's say the balloon is fine but then it comes down with alcoholism. It becomes excessively concerned with itself and because it's excessively concerned with itself, it's blowing a lot of air into itself. What happens to the skin of the balloon? It gets thinner, and if the skin gets too thin it could be popped (which would mean it's gauge of success would be doomed). So now, self centered fear arises and it says, "Jesus Christ, if my skin's gets too thin I could be easily popped." Now it's in a lot of fear and it starts looking around it's environment at what it thinks could pop it. (if its environment was a mental realm full of past and future, then there would be a whole lot more to be worried about) It doesn't matter if the thing can pop it or not, it only matters if it believes it can pop it. It's looking around and sees an exposed light and worries about touching that light because it will surely be a goner. It starts resenting that light, "Man, I wish that light wasn't there." A lit cigarette, same thing, ba boom--now it's resenting that cigarette. It's daily conditioning has become extreme self fear and resentment because now it is viewing everything as a possible threat. The more it applies its own solution to the problem of self-centeredness, the more it blows up. This is untreated alcoholism.

Its resentments and fears are based on its perception of outside situations. What would happen if the self-centeredness lessens? The skin gets thicker. The self centered fear starts diminishing, it doesn't see the light as having the ability to pop it because it's skin is thick enough to withstand it.

This is the mind of the alcoholic. Resentment and fear are being produced by where we are looking at things from. They are not happening from outside, they are being produced by where you are looking at life from. When you're obsessed with self, you're afraid you're not gonna get what you want, or lose what you have. Your entire life will be surveying what could possibly threaten your agenda.

There are not a thousand resentments out there. You produce the view of a threat by your perception. Fear is provoked by how you are looking at life.

It says in the *Big Book* of *Alcoholics Anonymous,* that the steps are to deflate the ego. When the air of self-importance is removed, the ego deflates to a right size and things look a lot different. It's all based on F.E.A.R.--false evidence appearing real. How could false evidence appear real unless it appears real to what is REAL?

Inventory

The inventory process is broken down into three manifestations of self. **Resentments,** (which means to re-feel), **fears** and **harms done to others. We look at the harms done to others specifically by looking at our behaviour concerning sex**. These are the three basic categories of the inventory process.

In step 3, *we made the decision* and all of those possibilities can be realized, but in order for them to stabilize, we need to do steps 4 through 9.

Taking Action

This program is not a program of thought, it's a program of action that revises the thought system. You cannot revise the thought system with the thought system. The thought system is revised through action. This is the program of *Alcoholics Anonymous.*

It's through action that the thought system changes, not through thinking. It's our interest and attention that gets released from the thought system which allows the Spiritual condition to become obvious.

The steps of AA, to me, diminish the mental condition which allows the Spiritual condition to become obvious.

Step Four

**Made a searching and fearless moral inventory of
ourselves.**
(Page 42-54, BB)

*Perhaps there is a better way - we think so. For we are
now on a different basis; the basis of trusting and
relying upon God. We trust infinite God rather than our
finite selves. (page 68 , BB)*

BB: *Being convinced that self, manifested in various ways, was
what had defeated us. We considered its common
manifestations. (page 64)*

Paul: This to me is one of the most important statements of
the book.   Convinced means to believe with certainty, and self
is that image that the mind has of you. It's through the
manifestations of self that we are defeated.   Then it says, *has
defeated us.*   So, it is separating the two, us and self. If you go
into a room full of people and you ask, "What self defeated
you?" Everyone would have the same answer, and it would be
'**my**' self. 'My' self defeated me. It's not self that defeats us, it's
the identification **as self** that opens us up to its defeat. If we are
not that, we can be free of its effects by not calling them ours.
How can self manifest so much in our life? It's in our
relationships, it goes into our ambition for our financial
security, it goes into our work life. How come it's splattering all
its effects throughout our life? Because every time it comes into

an aspect of our life, we call it 'me'. Basically, self is now expressing itself through us, by identification **as** it.

Resentment is the Number One Offender

BB: *Being convinced that self, manifested in various ways, was what had defeated us, we considered its common manifestations. Resentment is the number one offender. It destroys more alcoholics than anything else. From it, stems all forms of Spiritual disease, for we have been not only mentally and physically ill, we have been Spiritually sick. When the Spiritual malady is overcome, we straighten out mentally and physically. In dealing with resentments, we set them on paper. We listed people, institutions or principles with whom we were angry. We asked ourselves why we were angry. In most cases it was found that our self-esteem, our pocketbooks, our ambitions, our personal relationships (including sex) were hurt or threatened. So we were sore. We were "burned up."*

Paul: We're now gonna look at selfs common manifestation. It says in the beginning of the paragraph: *Resentment, if you look at it this way, resentment is an expression or manifestation of self in one's life. If you want to get rid of the resentment, get rid of where it comes from. It doesn't come from outside circumstances, it comes from self.*

Claiming to be the Doer

So, what we are suffering from are the manifestations of self and when people share about the manifestations of self they

80

usually claim it to be *theirs.* They say these are **my** resentments, they're **my** fears.

How are you going to be free from the disease if you keep claiming to be the doer of the disease? You've got to have the recognition that what is expressing through you, is not you.

If we are constantly claiming the expressions of self as mine, that is the activity of the root of the problem. Identification as self. If you were not identified as self, you would not claim the manifestations of self as yours. You would call them something else, you would call them fear--not **my** fear, you would call them resentment--not **my** resentment. We are talking from the problem about the solution, that's why there's no solution.

While I'm talking about the solution from the problem, that's a problem.

It's a Parasitical Movement

I'm not radically going to be free from the bondage of self if I keep claiming the expressions of self as *my own.* I have to get to a point where I hold an idea that this is a foreign installment, a parasitical movement that has presented itself as me. The way this life is to a parasite is the interpretation of it. My life is living. Its life is interpreting. It's a totally different way to go.

Living is spontaneous immediacy, its engaging. Interpreting is aloofness, it's separate, it's observing.

Instead of being in the football game, your attention is listening to the color commentator about the game. And it's comment is bias, it's not even close to what's happening. We are living in interpretation instead of living life. We have been seemingly taken over.

Life has been made into a still life. We know it before it's even going to happen, "Oh, I know what's it's going to be like when I go down to so and so's," "I know, I know," I mean, how dry do you want life to be? If it's that dry, you are going to be driven to seek relief.

In my community, I've never heard anyone express the inventory process as looking at the expressions of selfing in one's life. I always hear it as we're going to look at our resentment, our fears, our harming people. Maybe we cannot make that leap, so let them be called ours. Let's totally say these are my fears and my resentment and my harming others, but even if you totally take them on, they will eventually be seen as not being yours. You will have a true release from it. If you are trying to disavow them as yours, maybe it's best to sort of claim them totally as yours because, I'm telling you, inherently, they are not. They are self's. It is a foreign installment. He says it very clearly. Self and us, he separates the two. We are the us.

Money, sex, relationships, *my* money, *my* sex, *my* relationships; do you see the difference? If you do, the body is a body instead of my body. Then, feelings are just feelings instead of *my* feelings, stories are stories instead of *my* stories. Do you see the difference? Travelling heavy, includes the my. Travelling light, excludes the my.

We become afraid of living and we seek shelter in this false security of knowing. We live in the mind. We live in a safe space of interpretation,

but it's draining the life out of us.

Taking Action

So now we're going to take a look at doing the inventory starting with resentment.

BB: *Resentment is the number one offender, it kills more alcoholics than anything else.*
Paul: Harboring a resentment towards someone is a death knell in recovery. In one of the first editions of the *Big Book,* there's a great story by a woman named Wynn C. L. called "Freedom From Bondage." She got sober, but it was a rough road to finally get sober and she realized that if she did not get rid of her resentments she would probably drink again.

She had this one resentment. She had been telling herself that she would do anything to get rid of it. She said if she had a chance to get rid of it, she would have dropped it like a hot coal. It was about her mother, but when she got sober it was revealed to her that her mind was using that resentment toward her mother for an excuse about everything in life, about her failed marriages, about her not going to school; it was always about her mother. To her conditional mind, the selfing was like the golden cow. The last thing it wanted to let go of was this resentment. But all the while that she was under it, she was under an illusion that she would do anything to get rid of this resentment. Her mind had no intention of letting go of this golden cow. One day she was at a doctor's office and she saw a magazine and there was an article by a clergyman that said, "If you have a resentment and you can't seem to let go of it, try this." The advice was to pray for that person who you resent to have everything you want and more, even if you don't mean it. Do it for a few weeks and see what happens.

It works. It has been applied many times in my life. An example: I had this fairy princess; the first girl I fell for in AA. Feelings were invoked that I hadn't felt in years, since I was a kid, but I was unable to show up in the relationship. After a year-and-a-half, we broke up. One day I was at this day time party in Sausalito just hanging out there. (I had heard that she had met some other guy and was going to marry him.) Suddenly, she came in with this guy and it was like the sky opened up, they were beaming and everyone was looking at them like flower petals were being thrown in front of them. I was feeling a lot of anger towards her and towards him, an extreme amount of resentment. I left the party and I used that advice given by that clergyman, I used what they suggested because every time her name would come up in my head, I felt ill about her and her husband. I did it for a few weeks and you know what? It worked. That sour-ness left and ever since then, every time she's entered my mind, I feel a good feeling around it. This program of action works. You cannot think yourself out of the situation, but you can act yourself out of it.

Personal Inventory
(Pages 42 - 54 , BB)

Following, you will find the way that I was taught, that I find useful. I would suggest reading the *Big Book* for further discussion on this step. There are three inventories in Step 4:

Resentments, fear, and sexual inventory.

Inventory I
Resentment

The way I was taught to do the inventory is in a four column process where in the first column you write down a person, institution, or principal (like capitalism) that you resent (to re-feel). The second column is what happened; why are you resentful? In the third column, they use the idea of an instinctual agenda as the driving force in your life. For example: What's driving you to find a house is the *instinct to have shelter or to be taken care of.* All of our desires, activities and behaviors come from the basic instincts. They break down the instincts into: social aspect, pride, a sense of community, how people view you, emotional and material security. Material security is obviously having food, clothing and shelter. Emotional, is like having someone to love or having a family or animals or pets--something to engage in emotionally, and finally a sexual instinct. These instinctual drives are managed by self. Self is

85

directing, interpreting and managing the instincts. It's turning wants into needs.

The instinctual drives are the field where the self plays God. The fourth column would be, what was/is your role in things? They break those down into:

1. Where was or is there selfishness?
2. Where was or is there self seeking and frightened?
3. Where was or is there inconsideration?
4. Where was or is there dishonesty?

Remembering these are all expressions of **'self'** in one's life. These are **not** our expressions. Once you make the list, you can do 40 or 800 of them. Here is an example of what one resentment might look like, put into the process:

Wendy is my girlfriend. I resent her for leaving me. Wendy would be in the first column.

The second column would be, "Why am I pissed at her?" "She left me." Everybody in every bar does the first two columns of the inventory, they know who they are mad at and why. Yet it only leads to another drink.

The third column would be what was affected by her leaving me. What part of my instincts was affected? My personal relationships were affected. My pride, because I think I'm a ladies man, so my pride was affected because how could I be a ladies man if the lady leaves? How will other people view me? Now they're not viewing me like a ladies man so my social instinct was really affected by her leaving me. My financial security, because with her I was driving a BMW and now if she leaves, I'm driving a Pinto. I have to go back to my life and leave the nice place, this and that, so now, I'm super afraid and I'm trying to convince her not to leave me, not because I wanna be with her, but because I don't wanna lose what I have. Most people who are drunk, know who they are mad at (resentful) and why, but there is no solution in that. Their solution is to drink and be right. That doesn't work.

Our Program takes it to the fourth column and that is to look at ourselves. What is my role in it? Now, the light is off of Wendy and I'm looking at the selfishness and the self-centeredness and the fear.

I go through all the resentments in my life, taking it through every one of the columns and after a while, the information that I have been putting down starts to **show me the pattern of 'selfing'**.

I see how self has defeated me. I start to see what self takes to be really important. Whatever it deems to be important is where most of the fear and resentments are going to be.

Now I'm starting to see--not from the problem, but I can see the problem. I'm not calling it mine, but I am seeing it as something different than me; that's why I can be free of it. Just tell the truth about it.

Inventory II
Fear

BB: *We ask Him to remove our fear and direct our attention to what He would have us be.*

The second inventory is talked about on page 66-67 of the *Big Book*. This is the fear inventory. We do it the same way that we did with the resentments. (it's done with the columns)

In column one, I'm going to write down everything that I'm afraid of. In the second column, I'm going to write down why. The third column is where the fear is produced, being generated from the point of view of what was or would be affected. The fourth column is to see our role in it.

A lot of times you won't have any reason why you're afraid because the fear isn't coming from the outside. It's coming from how you're looking at it, not from what's happening outside. You don't even need a reason to be afraid. You might be thinking it may happen even if it's never happened but you're afraid it will. You do all of the columns the same way. This is just a different aspect or manifestation of self. **The manifestation of resentment seems to be coming from outside *at* you, the manifestation of fear comes from *in* you and then gets projected to the outside.** Resentment seems to attack you and fear is actually projected out. So you're actually looking at where you're coming from, not what's happening out there. With resentment, we follow the outside trail to get back to the inside, but in fear we start from the inside to look out.

BB: *This short word (fear) somehow touches about every aspect of our lives. It was an evil and corroding thread; the fabric of our existence was shot through with it.*

Paul: Let's say the fabric of my existence is blue and fear is a thread in this existence, and fear is blue. I'm going to have a very difficult time recognizing the fear from the fabric of my existence. It's become so ingrained that we don't know any better. We really don't.

Absence of Fear

Let's say when you were born, someone put a hand on your shoulder and it's been there ever since--you wouldn't know it was there. It would be producing effects, and you would be experiencing those effects but any idea of what was causing it would be off. You would have no idea that it was the reason why your shoulder bag doesn't stay up is because there is a hand on it. What happens when that hand is lifted? You would know it by its absence. You would go "Oh, that's why this sleeve was longer than the other sleeve, because I had this thing on me for my whole life."

You will know fear by its absence. When it's lifted, you will come to know it as misdirected faith. You will begin to be able to follow it to its source. You will know what has produced the anxiety and fear--self reliance. You will come to know it as faith. Fear is a valid emotion that appropriately arises in certain situations that command fight or flight. I think the word fear is being misapplied. I think that what we call fear is actually mental anxiety in most cases. Mental anxiety is mimicking the effects of fear as a reaction to what's not happening.

BB: *It (fear) sets in motion, trains of circumstances which brought us misfortune we felt we didn't deserve. But did not we, ourselves, set the ball rolling?*

Paul: This is like the skeletal diagram of the spiraling into a bottom. This is exactly how my life went. It, fear (false evidence appearing real) set in motion trains of circumstances which brought me misfortune, which I felt didn't deserve, which immediately brought me back to the fear because that which produces the fear which is self reliance was my condition. I went to the condition that produced the fear, to give me the solution to it. That set off more trains of circumstances, more misfortune, more undeserved resentment and self-pity; it was like a loop I could not get out of. The best I could do was get some relief in it, which was to get loaded. It only exacerbated the situation. But when there is no relief at hand, I'm going to grab whatever is available. You're in this self-centered loop and you can't get out of it and that imprint is becoming an expression. Your life is expressing the imprint of selfing in your head.

Hope That Restores

What *Alcoholics Anonymous* does, is it upsets or interrupts that loop. Instead of making decisions from self, you make decisions guided by the principals and the suggestions of the program, and for me, a lot of fortune started to happen that I felt I didn't deserve. My reaction was gratitude. You are now in the process of 'perhaps there is a better way,' **trusting something infinite rather than finite self.**

You go into your first meeting and they say: "Hey, come back tomorrow," and you say, "Okay, I'll come back," with the idea that it's going to keep me sober. Then they say, "Sit in the front and listen to the speaker." I say, "Okay, I hope you're right." Then they say, "Get a commitment, people who have commitments seem to stay sober." I say, "Okay, I hope you're right."

I started to make decisions based on hope on what was being suggested at the meetings. What happened was they set off trains of circumstances, but now those circumstances started to bring me fortune I feel I didn't deserve. What happens to me when I have fortune I feel like I don't deserve? I feel gratitude. I feel gratitude to what I believe brought me the fortune, which is the program. (God, Higher Power, etc.) The loop of self got broken by making a decision based on hope because I had no belief yet. I hadn't come to believe that something had restored me to sanity but I just took a chance, in a sense. What other chance did I have?

The hope very quickly turned into belief because it works. It's not a false advertising campaign. It actually produced relief. I wasn't drinking, I wasn't getting arrested, I found a place to live. The hope quickly changed to belief.

Life? Sometimes the circumstances bring me misfortune, but now I have the eyes to see the fortune in it. I can see the silver lining of a dark cloud. Before I would see the misfortune in fortune, now I see the fortune in misfortune. This process, starting off as a belief, turns into what? It turns into faith, which to me is the basis of emotional sobriety. Now I live in faith and feel as if I am in good hands, no matter the circumstance or situation.

More on Faith

Everyone has faith. Faith has a potential to manifest here by the vehicle it's put in. If you have faith in a failed system of thought, that faith is going to produce anxiety; you're going to be scared shitless because you're going to be affected by what's not happening all day. You're going to be worrying about some idea of being destitute next week or that your girlfriend is going to leave you because she sleeping with your best friend. It's not happening. Faith in the failed system produces anxiety.

The same faith put into centeredness produces an ease and comfort in your own skin. It's the exact same energy, it's just what it's put in. What is put in is determined by what's directing it.

What the program does is shift faith from a failed system and puts it into a reliable system.

It's like taking a rose bush that has the potential to bloom. It's in a small pot with lousy soil and not getting much water and no light. If it's self- centered, it's probably blaming itself for not blooming. It's probably thinking "I'm the only rose bush that cannot bloom, I'm so terrible." But if you took that rosebush and put it in a bigger pot with good soil, some water and light, it's going to freaking bloom. That's exactly what happens to the alcoholic if you take him out of the failed system and put them into a system that works. That addict that looked like it was going nowhere starts living an incredible life, contributing instead of taking. This is the beauty of this total radical shift of mind.

BB: *We reviewed our fears thoroughly. We put them on paper, even though we had no resentment in connection with them. We asked ourselves why we had them. Why do you have all this fear? Isn't it because self-reliance has failed you?*

Paul: This clearly states that the cause of fear in our life is reliance on self. Change the cause and you will change the effect. Changing the effects won't change the cause. Fear seems to produce a lot of effects, but what's producing the fear is self reliance. In my view there cannot be any higher form of self reliance than to be identified. I rely on a crutch but I don't think I am a crutch. Were so beyond obsession that we think we have obsessions.

The third inventory is the sexual inventory:

Inventory III
Sexual Inventory

This one has the same four columns with the addition of a fifth column which is: What I could have done instead.

Were trying to allow a new ideal to take precedence through the process of reviewing the first four columns and then asking what we could have done instead. It's because we're going to try to change our ideals about relationships by asking the question: What could I have done instead, with an intention of being willing to grow towards a new ideal concerning my relationships.

One of the main premises of the book is that when we are in alcoholism, we are incapable of having a viable relationship with another human being. We're so up the ass of self that we cannot connect. We cannot engage. You're so scared shitless to find out you're not right about someone that you won't even let them be what they are.

The first column are the people that I hurt. The second column is what did I do? Let's say I had an affair with a married woman so it affected her husband and the kids. Now their whole world is in turmoil. I played a role in that. So then I go to the third column and I look at my instinctual agenda to see what motivated me to do that. The instinctual drive was the motivator. The funny thing is I found in my sexual inventory that very rarely was I having sex for sex sake. I was having sex for self-esteem. I was in so much guilt and shame about how I was living that I had to convince myself that I was okay against tons of evidence that I wasn't.

A pretty women made me feel like I was okay, but not for long, I needed to meet more and different pretty women. It was becoming harder and harder to feel okay to the point where it just exhausted itself and the guilt and shame caught up with me. Thank God. That okayness usually expired quickly so I needed to get another signifier. The present signifier wasn't doing it, I had to go out and meet another one; not for the sex of it, but for the self esteem it produced.

It was another flavour of addiction. The weight of the guilt and the shame in how I was living was always bearing down on me and the drive and need to feel okay was becoming more and more necessary, yet the last signifier would expire quicker and quicker. It was like a drug. The only way I could feel okay out there with all the other evidence in my life, was if a parade of pretty women would go horizontal with me and then I would feel like I must be okay. Yet that sense of okayness didn't last. I had to go out again, to produce that okayness. It had to do with self esteem. Most of my acting out sexually had nothing to do with sex, it had to do with self esteem. I had to go out again and again.

So now I go to the fourth column and I look at where I was/am being selfish, self-centered and frightened. And if you have a big enough survey, you'll see the pattern of how self defeated you. The fifth column is to see how we would like to be by expressing or taking inventory of how we have been.

You'll see the pattern because the selfing, whatever it deems to be important, that's where it's minions show up. You start to see its effects, where it thinks something is important. You start recognizing through the manifestations, the theme of the self. Now you are getting back to the blueprint room, not the consequential state, and you're starting to see the beast from head to toe.

One of the main things that eventually hits you, is you are not that. That to me is the beginning of radical freedom. The mind, when identified with it, can never entertain being free *from* it. It can only entertain being free *as* it. Its ability to entertain is severely limited by being identified. It cannot entertain being free from it.That's why some people kill themselves. They don't drink again or use again but they want to shut that thing off, they can't separate themselves from it. They think it's them, so they kill themselves. To get some peace *from* it.

Instead of getting hit by the tail of the beast, you start seeing it from head to tail. One parasite with only a very limited amount of characteristics expressing through thousands of hosts and each host is speaking as if the parasite's characteristics are their own. That's the bondage of self. Each one of the hosts are calling the characteristics of the parasite their own. That's the bondage of self.

The fifth column of the sexual inventory.

Let's say I cheated on this woman. The question is simply, what could I have done instead? The obvious is not to cheat on her, yes? But a more subtle answer may be that I could have talked to someone before I went and did that. Basically you take a look at what you could have done which would have been opposite to what you did in the past, and you come up with a new ideal and ask for the willingness to live up to it. If you are willing to work toward that and you keep an eye on it, some power will flood into your life that will make it possible, or at least progress, toward that ideal. When I first got sober, I thought all I had to do was tell the woman my intention and if she agreed then everything was okay. Maybe I would tell her that I wanted to have just a relaxed engagement and she would agree and I would go for it, and the shit would hit the fan. Then the honesty started to change a little bit and I learned to read her--maybe she was saying yes, but emotionally she couldn't have a casual sexual relationship or maybe I couldn't. So, I knew I had to pass on that, that I had to have more responsibility with what I was doing. That's what happened when I did the inventory. I saw my ideals and I lived up to them as best as I could. My relationships have changed dramatically to the point where I really don't have one.

Summary

The fourth and the tenth step are both inventories. The fourth step is like a major house cleaning and the 10th step is continuing to take inventory. The 10th step is more about tidying up so you don't get all the shit built up. Some people say you do the steps once, other people say you re-engage with them. There's no set way, it's all interpreted from the people who are doing them.

Step Five

**Admitted to God, to ourselves, and to another human being
the exact nature of our wrongs.**
(Page 72, BB)

This is what happens. You finish your 4th step and you find someone who you trust. It could be some member in the program, or outside, it doesn't matter; it's up to you. This is sort of like a trinity. **It cannot be done with one of these things missing.**

It needs to be you, the Higher Power (how you understand it) and another person.

The other person holds the space to hear your inventory. If you try to do it yourself with your God, without the person, or if you try to just do it with a person without a Higher Power, it's not going to produce the same result.

That's why it's good to follow the 12 steps as they are presented. It's like a soup mix. If you just follow the instructions, it will produce the soup that it says on the label. If you try to shortcut or add something to it you may not get what was advertised, which is a freedom from the obsession to drink one day at a time.

When I did my first inventory, I found that one of the most important things in Step 5 was that I had a secret I never told anybody. It was something that I was doing when I was young and I had a lot of guilt and shame about it, but I kept doing it. I never shared it with anybody and I really had no intention of ever sharing it with anyone. It was going to stay in that little vault and I would pay the security guards that had, to watch it for the rest of my life.

One of the biggest events in my fifth step was when I shared it. The funny thing is when I shared it, the guy missed it. He was yawning and didn't hear it. I actually said it twice in one day, when I swore I would never say it to anyone. And you know what? It was not a big deal to him. That's the beauty about things. If they are kept in the head, they can be really, really big. But if you share them with another they become right sized.

That's the thing about the fourth step; that four column inventory can hold the heaviest thing that's in your head; and in your heart; it can hold the heaviest thing that you've been carrying around for so many years; it can hold it all, and the paper will not collapse. The beauty about the fourth step and the whole process is that it will produce an answer, **but it won't be your answer**. Now you're going through processing life with a different processor because the old one is broken.

The *12 Steps of Alcoholics Anonymous,* gave me some sound principles that can replace the failed strategies of my mind. What ends up occurring is, over time, you will see that you're traveling a lot lighter and you will be able to deal with life on life's terms.

In a sense, when I drank, I didn't have a drinking problem, I had a living problem. I could not handle life on life's terms. It overwhelmed me. I just did not want to show up. Drinking and drug use helped me to make it through, seemingly, that was my solution to the dilemma.

You'll have a new attitude and a new outlook and you will know peace and comprehend serenity (The Promises, page 84 BB) In other words, things will be really fresh and new. The old will be thrown out and the new will replace it.

When I did the fifth step, and told that guy the secret, that was an incredible amount of relief. As I was sharing, my sponsor pointed out some basic themes of the selfing. When he was pointing that out, it made some big impacts, like the idea of most of my sexual behavior was really about self esteem, not sex. Also a lot of my fears about certain topics like finance had nothing to do with finance, they had to do with pride and what I felt other people were going to think about me.

The dispersal started to happen and I could see the effects and a lot of things got undone by following them back to the cause which was always selfishness, self-seeking and fear. As I continued, the same old behaviors would come up and I now recognized them **as** they were coming up. Where before, I recognized them days or months later, or sometimes never recognized them.

The Pause (see page 27)

A miraculous event started to happen more frequently. What we call the 'pause,' became a new possibility. Instead of almost no time between a thought turning into an action, suddenly there was this gap or pause which allowed a new direction. Instead of always going down the same old same old, new possibilities appeared. Old strains of deep mental grooves, some I never thought I would be freed from, suddenly were preceded by a pause which allowed that old behavioral pattern to stop and a new one to start to grow.

In my experience the pause is like a timeless moment in a moment in time.

It's what makes a new happiness and a new freedom possible.

The pause was the first sighting of what I really am in this action figure life.

What occurred, is I was provided by Grace the ability to have a pause. Before, when these knee-jerk behavioral patterns would arise, I'd be off and running, and after all the consequences, the ruminating wound follow. Now, before they could find expression through me, they were stopped and they couldn't get any traction in a pause. A lot of times what occurred was the pause was a timeless moment in time, and that pause allowed the possibility for anything to change. Deep mental grooves, that would always jackpot me, when preceded by a pause, could be totally nulled. It's an incredible power. At first it was about seeing the patterns, but they were still happening, but I could see the patterns as they were happening; I could see the patterns begin to form before they happened and at that point there was freedom from the pattern.

Before recovery, I was on the consequential level. Things were happening and I had no idea why and I couldn't follow any effect to its cause; I was sort of in the dark just getting whacked. It was so bad that I would go out at times and I would go to a bar, shoot some pool, start drinking, cop some drugs and go out dancing. My intentions seemed to be that I wanted to have fun. Then, by around 12:30 I'd be invited to the police station. I'd get out the next day and the next night I would go out and do the same thing. I'd get arrested again and be incredibly surprised that it happened. Yet I had done exactly what I did two nights ago to get me in jail. This is the definition of insanity. In recovery it gets illuminated. It's through Illumination that it changes.

After a while, if enough gets illuminated you may see that you are the illumination; you're the light in your own life. It may not go that far, but it is a possibility.

I had done the fifth step and was seeing these patterns and getting quicker and quicker to the point where I was in the blueprint room instead of being the effects of the patterns.

A whole new basis of living was starting to become available and what was happening in my life was different, really different. After months of recovery, I was starting to have a feeling I couldn't put my finger on. I finally realized what it was, it was a sense of belonging. AA was now providing things I needed that I had no idea I needed.

A power greater than me was doing for me what I could not do for myself. A great gift is when you can actually do a fifth step with someone else, because the steps are seen quite differently when you are leading someone through them than when you were doing them yourself. The fifth step, the privilege of being able to hold the space for a person, to be all the things that they are not, is a very, very, great honor.

Nearer to Step Six

God, help me become willing to let go of all the things to which I still cling.

Help me to be ready to let You remove all of these defects, that Your will and purpose may take their place.

Amen
(BB, page 76)

Step Six

Were entirely ready to have God remove all these defects of character.
(Page 76, BB)

Step 6 & 7 are not something you do and then you're done with them. They continue to happen because more gets revealed.

The fourth step is putting down on paper how self defeated us.

The fifth step is sharing it, which opens up the possibility of seeing the patterns more clearly on how self defeated us.

The sixth step is what you do when you start seeing the patterns.

At this point, you are entirely ready to have God remove all of the defects of character. Before the process of the steps, there was a lack of awareness of the causes, conditions and exact nature of the wrongs. **Now you are seeing and when you do, you state that you are entirely ready to have God remove all of these defects of character.**

Step 7 is humbly asking that Power to remove them.

Recognizing the garbage and putting it out the night before the garbage man is scheduled to come is how far you carry the ball. Not you, but the garbage man takes care of the garbage. You run as far as you can and then you put the ball down and something else picks it up and takes it away. In step 6, there is a willingness, and step 7 is a request and that's the end of your job. That's called trusting the process. You don't sit up all night, looking for the garbage man. You go to bed, rest assured that the garbage will be gone the next morning.

If you can have faith in the garbage man, why can't you have faith in God.

Before, you were not seeing the defects; now you're seeing them, you are seeing the expressions of self. Now you are ready to have these things removed because first you needed to know that they were there. If I had a house and I didn't think it had any furniture, why would I order a moving van? Once I started waking up and realizing that I had all this stuff in my house, then the moving van becomes valuable. To become entirely ready? You'll never know when you're entirely ready. You will know when you're entirely ready when that which you're entirely ready to have removed is removed. Then you will know it. A lot of times, what you think needs to be removed is not going to be removed because it has a purpose. That's because something is running you now and it has a grander plan for your life then you. So, some of what you call your defects can be very helpful in helping other people. They're not going anywhere. That's because something is going to speak to others, as you, through you, by you. That's what I discovered very quickly in AA. Basically all of the changes are about maximizing your usefulness. The goals of the steps are not a me-oriented goal, they are a we-oriented goal. The point is to become of maximum use to those you would help.

There is a famous prayer: (page 63, BB)

God, I offer myself to Thee-to build with me and to do with me as Thou wilt. Relieve me of the bondage of self, that I may better do Thy will. Take away my difficulties, that victory over them may bear witness to those I would help of Thy Power, Thy Love, and Thy Way of life. May I do Thy will always!

If you are willing to be a hose, this water will come through. There's a statement in *Alcoholics Anonymous*, that I don't agree with and that is that you have to have it to give it away. I don't believe so. I believe that if you are willing to give it away, you'll have it. It will move through you. That's been my experience. I've heard some incredibly wise stuff coming from a newcomer. That wasn't something that they had acquired or claimed, it just came through them because of the circumstances; the message needed to be heard by another person. You see that you're a much bigger piece of the game board than you think.

Step 6 is obviously an ongoing step because a lot more gets revealed. It's the living that provokes the stuff and then you get to see it and then there comes a point of being entirely ready to have it removed and then it seems to be removed, unless there's a larger purpose for it.

Not Yet Step Seven

My Creator

I am now willing that You should have all of me, good and bad.
I pray that you now remove from me every single defect of
character
which stands in the way of my usefulness to You and my
fellows.
Grant me strength as I go out from here to do Your bidding.

Amen

Faith without works is dead.
(BB)

Step Seven

Humbly asked Him to remove our shortcomings.
(Page 76, BB)

Steps 4 & 5 brought to light the defects of character. Step 6 is that you are entirely ready to have them removed, and Step 7 is to humbly ask that Power to remove them.

In the living of life, the defects will come up and we get to see them in the light. There has been a recognition of the defects in steps 4 and 5 so when they appear in life, there is a recognition now because of what was revealed. So when it appears again in your life, there is an ah-ha, a dawning, and then the idea of readiness for things to be removed.

Sometimes you realize there's not a readiness for anything to be removed because of the identification as self, the one who has the defects of character. You realize that the story of you doing anything to be rid of them, is just flat out not true. The selfing may find great value in what you keep professing you'd love to lose. You can notice that there is an extreme disconnect to what is actually happening and what you think is happening. Your values that you profess so authentically may actually be the values of the selfing. The selfing may allow you to have your story, but in that, it's actually having you. The only thing power respects is a greater power. The greater power's influence has been co- opted through identification so now the lesser power is taken to be the greater power by the lesser power. In this seeming condition the introduction to a Higher Power aka 'you' may be 'seen' as something other than you--given a name, The Higher Power.

Right Before Step Eight

The idea of acceptance is really big in *Alcoholics Anonymous.* To me, acceptance is sort of an attitude or an outlook that is a by-product of the psychic change. In selfing, you cannot have acceptance because you may call it acceptance but it's usually tolerance. There's a set timetable that when it runs out, the tolerance will turn into intolerance.

In time, acceptance becomes infused in your attitude and outlook. Some things are unacceptable, yet there will be an acceptance of things.

Step Eight

**Made a list of all persons we had harmed, and became
willing to make amends to them all.**
(Page 77, BB)

The material that made up the fourth step is what is used to
write your 8th step list, yet a lot of people that you have
harmed will not fall under the category. A lot of people that
you have harmed will not fall under the category of fear,
resentment, or sex. If I robbed a liquor store, I may not have
resented them, I didn't have sex with anyone there and they
didn't provoke any fear, I just needed money. So, I harmed the
owners and needed to make an amends.

This step is simply making a list of the people that you've
harmed in your past through the selfing. That's it. You make a
list. Honesty is such an important aspect of this program, the
honesty and the humility will facilitate some real shifting.

Step 8, is making a list of people you have harmed. Just do it.

**If you would like to know the essence of this book, please
refer to page 27.**

Stepping Up to Step Nine

In selfing, one of the main foundations is to be the personal doer in life. There are many statements in Spirituality; one by Lord Buddha saying "Events happen, deeds are done, but there is no individual doer therof." But in selfing, the feeling of being the doer is paramount. In that sense of being the doer, there is a big branch for guilt and shame to nest.

The movement of selfing is to claim. The selfing claims the action and uses all the actions to imply the actor. In the seeming condition of the bondage of self, this is like the crazy glue. **The sense of personal doership is the basis of the self story. If these actions weren't yours, whose life would it be anyway? This, the selfing will not tolerate. You can speak about not being the seer, the hearer, the feeler, but when you talk about not being the doer, that shakes up the applecart.**

In the first step there is an admittance of us being powerless over alcohol. It would be like when you're dancing with a gorilla, you're gonna stop dancing when the gorilla wants to stop. As an alcoholic and a drug addict, I had lost my ability to control my using and drinking. This loss of control put me under the control of the parasite. At this point I was basically being used for transportation; a vehicle of expression. I didn't know what was going to happen because something had me. The behaviour that happened under the influence had nothing to do with volition, it had to do with possession; yet still, the freedom from guilt and shame, based on 'my actions' while under the influence, are still being used to generate guilt and shame now, for that which happened in the past.

Yet, wasn't I powerless? Under the influence of the parasite, how responsible was I for the actions that occurred? There will be no freedom or forgiveness for the actor of those actions if I have been identified as being the doer, I will still be identified with what was done. How can there be freedom in that? You were used to do many, many things. We are accountable for the effects, but are we truly responsible?

We were used against our will.

To have access to God, which I need in this life, while relying on an unreliable system called self-centeredness is insanity to me. If the access point is always available at all times, with no requirement necessary to meet it, wouldn't it seem very reliable?

When life is happening, there's a flow with that. From selfing, life is seen as happening to me. From there, a lot of opinions and objections will arise about what's happening, which should or should not be happening to me. Selfing begets more selfing. In identification, we can only try to become what we already are. In the seeing of what you are not (self) is the finding out of what you are.

You can not know what you are, you can only be what you are.

In identifying as what you are not, what you are gets objectified. You start looking for you. From this point we will now believe we can do and have ourselves into being. All the while the trying to do and have ourselves into what we are, hides the fact that we are that. Starting at Being, doing and having is seen as an expression, not a vehicle to arrive at.

Step Nine

**Made direct amends to such people wherever possible,
except when to do so would injure them or others.**
(Page 83-84, BB)

Step 9, was a huge one for me. It really produced a lot of effects because there was so much guilt and shame in my life for what I thought I had done.

Step 9 Promises:

BB: If we are painstaking about this phase of our development, we will be amazed before we are halfway through. We are going to know a new freedom and a new happiness. We will not regret the past nor wish to shut the door on it.
Paul: I'll tell you, in selfing, one of the biggest attractions is the past. There is no self. For self to appear, it has to be remembered. Its logic goes like this: "I was there, I will be there, therefore I am now."

Concern and speculation about the future is another form of remembering self, now. Remembering is not just the past, you're being remembered in the future. There is no self without past or future; self is of time and time is of self. So many feelings we have now are truly being generated from the preoccupation with the past. We have an engraved seat in the first row at the movie *Life With Paul*. It's 'watching' all of the things you've done, all the things you've omitted or committed and man it goes on and on and on. To have this sense of not regretting the past nor shutting the door on it, is truly freeing!

BB: *We will comprehend the word serenity and we will know peace.*

Paul: This statement is a description of an effect that comes about through doing the steps. By this time, The predominant mental state has been diminished and qualities and characteristics of the Spiritual state (the Spiritual condition, centeredness) are rising to the top. When the mental state is diminished, the possibility of a Spiritual state starts becoming obvious and is known by its expressions such as peace and serenity. A new music station is now playing through the radio. Seems like the same old radio, but it is playing a new tune. How can that be serenity and peace if you are in a state of agitation? What is the mind in selfing? It's the state of desiring to become what it never can be and unbecome what it thinks it is. That means it's in a constant state of agitation. It's constantly appearing to be a self to us but can never become a self.

You finally get it. You finally get the flavor of it. Just like I was given the surrender, it's the same thing. I was given the taste of serenity, now I can comprehend it. I was given the taste of peace, now I can know peace. I couldn't know it before, because of the knower.

BB: *No matter how far down the scale we have gone, we will see how our experience can benefit others.*

Paul: For years, before I got sober, I truly believed that everything that I did every day had no value. I was just a parasite running around like a rat, trying to get that cheese of drugs and alcohol. That was my judgment of it. I surrendered my life and will through this program, to a Higher Power. This program, like the great recycler it is, took what I called a wasted life and has continued to mine great value out of it. What you would throw away, will be greatly used by a Higher Power. The value of surrender in time is rooted in what you surrender to. I had surrendered many times in life to the police, drugs, women and my head. Different effects were produced based on what was surrendered to. In my own experience, the turning over one's will and life over to the care of a Higher Power through the program of recovery has produced the greatest effects and continues to this day.

BB: *That feeling of uselessness and self pity will disappear.*

Paul: It doesn't say that you did anything to make it disappear. It will disappear. *We will lose interest in selfish things and gain interest in our fellows. Self-seeking will slip away.* These are all effects of the psychic change.

BB: *Our whole attitude and outlook upon life will change. Fear of people and of economic insecurity will leave us.*

Paul: The funny thing with the *Big Book* is, every description of the problem--I identified with. Every description of the effects of the solution--I identify with. I've never run into a book that I have constant comprehensive experience of what they say, a sense felt intimacy of both the bad and the good. *We will not regret the past nor wish to shut the door on it*---that comes from Step 9; that's when it started to set up. *We are going to know a New Freedom and happiness*--that has been with me since step 3. *We will comprehend the word serenity and we will know peace*--these are just expressions that arise from doing the steps.

You comprehend the word serenity by having serenity. You recognize peace from peace. The old mind-set has been weakened and now possibilities that were not available, are. What seemed to have been withheld is now open to you. Once you get a sense of what serenity is, you can entertain it. Once you get a sense of peace, you can entertain it.

Please remember, we're always going to be used as the action figure. The joy of being used and the hell of being used is determined by what's using you. These effects are not for you, they are gonna be used for others, through you. I have been used, just as I am, to help other people, and other people have been used to help me over and over again in this community. Once you see that you are of use, that sense of uselessness will disappear.

This program diminishes a mental condition, bringing out what is always there. Self as the dominant condition, entertains the idea it can be in self and out of self yet always claiming to be the 'one' that is out or in.

In seeing you are not that which claims to be the one 'in' or 'out,' that's the state of being out of self.

The only reason why you were trying to get out of self is you thought you *were* one. That was what was driving the desire to get out of it. When you realize that you are not that, the desire to get out of it gets dismissed because you were never in it. That is the experience of what you would call being out of self.

It frees you because you were never bound.

The freedom doesn't come from finally being released; just realizing you were never bound, that's the freedom. It is always available at all times, right where you are with no requirements to meet it, except the ones that you believe.

When I first came into AA, I had to do things to provoke gratitude, like gratitude lists and service. Now the attitude is infused with gratitude. What I used to call having an experience of gratitude is now a state. It's the way I'm lived.

Regarding economic security, a lot of people get mixed up. They think that they will now have money or something. It's not that your economic condition is going to change (though it may), it's the fear around it that will change. Fear finding expression is more about you than what seems to be happening. Self-reliance is the activator of fear and its expression is mental anxiety.

More on Fear

The fear becomes the producer of the threat instead of a reaction to a threat. The looking based on fear is seeing threats. The mental anxiety uses the past and the future to fan the flame of fear, now. It's not what's happening that's fanning the flame, it's the preoccupation of what's not happening that fans the flame of fear.

As the *Big Book* states: *We manufacture our own misery.* Where is the factory? **It's in yesterday and tomorrow.** And can't you literally say that that's not happening? If the cause of the problem is not happening, what more do you need to do than to see that?

If I went to a therapist, and the first thing that they said to me was that what's driving you crazy is not happening, that would be the end of the session. What more can I do? Do I want to talk about what's not happening? No, because then it would seem to be happening again? The solution is a recognition that it's not happening.

The instinctual drives will still be there, but what will be directing the instinctual drive will be different. You will know the tree by its fruits. That's that.

Once the sense of ownership is weakened through the third step, then you will know by its absence, that your managing was the unmanageability. How you travel now changes dramatically.

The sense of ownership--the sense of mine, me, my--is the activity, is the problem. You know the problem by the solution. In the solution there is no problem. By the problem's absence, you'll know the solution and the solution will inform you of the problem. You'll know what was seemingly stopping the possibility of relief, when the relief shows up.

BB: *We will intuitively know how to handle situations which used to baffle us. We will suddenly realize that God is doing for us what we could not do for ourselves.*

Paul: This is observing the effects of the solution. Instead of being the effects of a problem, we are now expressing the effects of the solution. **The I was, The I will be, is nullified by the I AM.**

BB: *Are these extravagant promises? We think not. They are being fulfilled among us—sometimes quickly, sometimes slowly. They will always materialize if we work for them.*

Paul: When the promises are received, they are definitely extravagant. We are now the expression of the solution just as we were the expression of the problem.

This concludes the ninth step promises.

The ninth step in action:

I got run over, twice in one night by a car. After about a year of recovery I moved to California and started to act out just like I was before. Many times when I was using I ran into patches where I didn't have much money. For dealers to front me drugs I would tell them a story about how I was going to get this large settlement for getting run over. That I would pay them when I got the money. I went on and on doing all the shit I was doing, and to sort of balance that guilt and shame, I swore to myself that I would give my mother money when I got the settlement.

This went on for years. I finally got the settlement, which was not even close to what I was expecting. I went back to New York, where my mother lived and where I got run over to pick up the settlement, and immediately bought as much cocaine as I could. I drove out to the end of Long Island to a town called West Hampton. The route I took went right by where my mother was living. I drove right by the turn off and went my very unmerry way to a rendezvous with pitiful, incomprehensible demoralization.

I spent all that money. $35,000 on drugs and after five weeks, there was no money and no drugs. Every non-drug thing I bought in those five weeks was lost and or stolen. I had nothing to show for it except an unquenchable desire. There is nothing like having a lot of cocaine and then having no cocaine. The agony of that desire not being met has no hellish bounds. Constantly going over this after the fact of disappointing my mother, was one of those things that I could not see any escape from. When I got sober, my mother was so happy that I was sober and through getting the first step I realized that what I 'did' to my mother, I would have done to anybody. Through realizing that what I had was a disease and not a problem of lack of will, I found forgiveness where I could not find forgiveness.

As an example of what it's like to be carrying around this stuff: I got sober in San Francisco. There was an area in San Francisco called North Beach and there were some really good meetings over there. Anyone who knows San Francisco knows that parking is at a premium. We would drive to North Beach to go to the meeting and there was a place that I would never go near, it was an entire block that I wouldn't go by. I didn't want to park there because there was this market called Rossi's Market. When I was living there in North Beach, I used to steal every day from that store. I would wear those long coats and I would slip two 16 ounce beers and a steak in my back. I did it for months every day and never got caught. Now that I was starting to become conscious, I didn't want to go see Rossi's Market, so I would never go down that road. You see, Rossi's Market was taking up a lot of space in my head. This went on for a couple of months until finally I decided I was going to go and confront that situation. I walked in and I asked one of the counter people where I could find the manager and he said "He's up in that booth." So, I went up the stairs and knocked on the door. The guy opened up and I told him that I used to live around there, that I was in a program of recovery and part of it had to do with making amends. I told him that I used to steal a lot from the store and that I wanted to give him some money. It wasn't much, but I gave him $55. I walked out and left. The funny thing is, I've never thought of Rossi's Market again. That's the beauty of amends.

The way I used to process life was not on life's terms. I tried to fit everything around me and never tried to fit myself around circumstances. I avoided, put off, denied, rationalized everything and anything. If my right arm was bleeding, I would look left all day.

Here's another example that captures the theme of how I rolled: I had gotten into some trouble that ended up with me having a court date for October 10th. One week before the date; I started to worry. Anxiety started to build because I believed if I went to the court date, l may end up in jail. This concern was not unfounded because many times I ended up in jail after a court appearance. Relying on self, I went to the mental Greek oracle and asked "Oh wise one what should I do?" As always the mental state freely gave me its advice and that was "Don't go to the court date." I didn't. What a relief. I was freed from the fear. October 10th found me in my apartment drinking and feeling quite superior to all those other jamokes that were sweating out their day in court. A few days pass. I'm driving my girlfriend's car and the police pull me over. Feeling confident that I haven't done anything wrong, I felt pretty assured it was gonna go alright. What always amazed me when I got pulled over is how long they would stay in their car before they come up to your car. When they knock on your window and you hear this statement, it means you're going to jail. "Mr. Hedderman, will you please step out of the car." At this point, I became pretty irate because I hadn't done anything wrong and I started to argue with the policeman, and I asked him why he stopped me. He said I had a broken tail light. I asked why he was taking me to jail, and he said they have bench warrant out for my arrest. I said "What's that?" He says "You missed the court date, so you're going to jail." Two weeks before this happened, when I was attempting to deal with the fear of going to jail that I felt the court date implied, my head came up with the great idea not go to the court date, therefore there would be no fear of going to jail. Now, I'm in jail with two court dates. That's the story of my life. I'm afraid to go to jail and I follow my mental instructions and I end up in jail, with two court dates. It's a reverse fishes and loaves. All I started off with was a court date. Under my head's jurisdiction the court date was implying that I am going to jail. I don't want to go to jail, hence the solution, don't go to the court date. Eureka, the fear disappeared temporarily, only to increase itself more from the exact thing I was trying to avoid.

Failed GPS

A blow by blow account of my life being led by this crazy failed GPS. I would be sitting in my apartment and I like to be happy and feel good and I ask my GPS to download some apps on how to navigate this night and arrive at some fun and excitement. The basic theme of all the requests. This is what got downloaded: It would lead me to a bar; I would drink. Shortly, that would not be enough. I would cop drugs, look for women, go dancing; so far so good. But now my big plan and design gets rudely interrupted by a person or persons in uniform. Then I was brought to their destination for me which is jail. I get out the next day and still relying on the same failed system, starting to get irritable restless and discontent as night falls, I turn to my GPS once again putting in a simple request... Have some fun, have a nice time, meet somebody, and around 12--12:30, I'd end up in jail again. Years of relying on a system that produces these effects. Maybe now you will be able to capture the urgency I was constantly in to get relief from that--self.

I would forget court dates but the courts didn't. I'd forget I owed money but the people I owed money to didn't. If my left arm was bleeding, I would just look right. Living on the edge wasn't doing drugs and running wild. What scared me the most would be the idea of going to a job interview or dealing with unconditional love. That scared the hell out of me. Saddled with this M.O., it's not surprising that there would be so much wreckage in one's life. There's a statement in AA, "Any life run on self will, will hardly be a success."

The 9th step is the way of cleaning up a lot of the mess of the past and getting freed from the past without shutting the door on it or regretting it.

When I was first in AA, there was no way in hell that I was going to do the ninth step. As I continued to do the first eight steps, when I arrived at step 9, I was quite ready to make the amends.

This is a process, like a soup mix and it actually works. It will distill all the alcoholism out of you. It can, if you are entirely ready for that. Then you'll be free from alcoholism, a day at a time.

I was the youngest of four. My oldest sister killed herself at 40 something years old. She turned into an alcoholic in her late thirties and she overdosed on pills after her marriage collapsed. I had witnessed some of that decline. My older brother killed himself also and my younger sister had a lot of trouble when she was young, but she sort of straightened out.

I was just a royal pain in the ass, so my mother went through a whole lot of hell with her biological connection with these four action figures. All she wanted was for me to be okay. She would send me these Saint Jude medals, who was the Patron Saint of lost souls, and these cards, and she had all these people praying for me. Maybe it worked, because I got sober. She was busily trying to do whatever she could to send some good mojo toward me. I got sober two years before she died and I'm so happy about that because I got to make amends to her. There's no way I could have made amends for every particular thing I ever participated in but I could make a living amend. It's one of the biggest things we do in recovery. There's no way to produce a value that would measure up to what we seem to have done to people. But we can reach a point where we won't do it to anyone else. That's called a living amend.

That living amend was an amazing gift for me and for my mother because there was so much stuff that had happened. I had storage units of guilt and shame. Now my heart's come back where I can see how my behavior and actions can affect others. Back then, the self-centeredness was so dominant that I had no idea how people were feeling about my behavior nor did I seem to care about it at all.

So the 9th Step for me was very, very freeing. The funny thing that happened is a lot of the people I had successfully been avoiding for many many years I suddenly kept running into all of them. My knee jerk reaction when I saw them was to turn left, but AA had a hold of me. I stopped and walked right up to them and would apologize or give them money, whatever was appropriate. There were some that I couldn't find, so I just wrote letters to them because I was willing to make the amends. That's the most important part, is to be willing to go to any lengths. The length you may be asked to go may be very short, you may not be asked to do much. The important point is the willingness. I was willing to confront the people that I had harmed, show up, tell the truth and clean up the mess. You cannot know how much the past dominates you until you are freed from it.

BB: *If we are painstaking about this phase of our development...*

Paul: The painstaking phase of the program is steps 4 thru 9--that's the phase of my development, those are the action steps.

BB: We will be amazed before we are halfway through. We are going to know a New Freedom and a new happiness and we have ceased fighting anything or anyone-even alcohol. For by this time, sanity will have returned. We will seldom be interested in liquor. If tempted, we recoil from it as from a hot flame. We react sanely and normally, and we will find that this has happened automatically. We will see that our new attitude toward liquor has been given us without any thought or effort on our part. It just comes! That is the miracle of it.

Paul: At this point, doing and having has been dismissed. What the steps have done to you allows all these effects to become possible. We do not produce the effects, we become a vehicle for them to express through. There is a point where you're running with the ball and a point where you put the ball down. Something else picks the ball up and carries it all the way, we don't.

BB: We will see that our new attitude toward liquor..

Paul: Or our new attitude towards men, women, money or time. This is basically saying that your role is finished, you're not fighting it, you're not trying to be vigilant, you're not trying to fix anything. This is just an effect that's having a chance to express through us. It doesn't need your help. You're just there to witness it and to live through its expression.

Toward Step Ten

The *Big Book,* page 85

It is easy to let up on the Spiritual program of action and rest on our laurels.

We are headed for trouble if we do, for alcohol is a subtle foe. We are not cured of alcoholism.

What we really have is a daily reprieve contingent on the maintenance of our Spiritual condition.

Every day is a day when we must carry the vision of God's will into all of our activities.

How can I best serve Thee - Thy will (not mine) be done.

These are thoughts which must go with us constantly.

We can exercise our willpower along this line all we wish.

It is the proper use of the will.

Step Ten

Continued to take personal inventory and when we were wrong promptly admitted it.
(Page 84, BB)

This thought brings us to *Step 10*, which suggests we continue to take personal inventory and continue to set right any new mistakes as we go along. We vigorously commenced this way of living as we cleaned up the past. We have entered the world of the Spirit. Our next function is to grow in understanding and effectiveness. This is not an overnight matter. It should continue for our lifetime. Continue to watch for selfishness, dishonesty, resentment, and fear. When these crop up, we ask God at once to remove them. We discuss them with someone immediately and make amends quickly if we have harmed anyone. Then we resolutely turn our thoughts to someone we can help.

Love and tolerance of others is our code.

BB: We have ceased fighting anything or anyone - even alcohol. For by this time sanity will have returned. We will seldom be interested in liquor. If tempted, we recoil from it as from a hot flame. We react sanely and normally, and we will find that this has happened automatically. We will see that our new attitude toward liquor has been given us without any thought or effort on

131

our part. It just comes! That is the miracle of it. We are not fighting it, neither are we avoiding temptation. We feel as though we had been placed in a position of neutrality - safe and protected. We have not even sworn off. Instead, the problem has been removed. It does not exist for us. We are neither cocky nor are we afraid. That is our experience. That is how we react so long as we keep in fit Spiritual condition.

It is easy to let up on the Spiritual program of action and rest on our laurels. We are headed for trouble if we do, for alcohol is a subtle foe. We are not cured of alcoholism. What we really have is a daily reprieve contingent on the maintenance of our Spiritual condition. Every day is a day when we must carry the vision of God's will into all of our activities. "How can I best serve Thee - Thy will (not mine) be done." These are thoughts which must go with us constantly. We can exercise our willpower along this line all we wish. It is the proper use of will.

Much has already been said about receiving strength, inspiration, and direction from Him who has all knowledge and power. If we have carefully followed directions, we have begun to sense the flow of His Spirit into us. To some extent we have become God-conscious. We have begun to develop this vital sixth sense. But we must go further and that means more action.

Paul: This is exactly how I feel, and I have never even met this guy. This was 1939 when it was written. How can you have such an incredible way of expressing the relief from alcoholism? How can I be so clearly identified with the same results? It's because we're getting relief from the same thing. A foreign installment, a parasitical system of thought called alcoholism. We are like all like hosts that have been freed from the same parasite. So when one host gets freed, it sure sounds like the same freedom I'm having. At this point, it's not inherent freedom, it's freedom *from*. Freedom from this parasite.

BB: *We have not even sworn off. Instead, the problem has been removed.*

Paul: Now, that is a damn good solution.

BB: *It does not exist for us.*

Paul: For the relief to stabilize, it has to progress to 'The problem does not exist as us'. Now that's incredible, when you recognize that something that had such influence doesn't exist anymore. When you can truly see it as non- existent; it shifts its influence greatly. As long as you are giving it credence as something real, it has you, now when you see that it doesn't exist for you, that's freedom. When you see that it doesn't exist AS you, that's a radical freedom.

How it stabilized with me is that it doesn't exist as me. I'll take it to be me if the identification of self is still in place. It may have periods where the problem doesn't exist for you but they will just be periods. But if it doesn't exist as you because you've seen the root of the problem is identification as, if you recognize that you are not that as, you are not a *self*--now the problem doesn't exist as you. This causes the experience of it not existing for you to become a state. It now does not exist as you. When it doesn't exist *for* you, it's still not on a solid foundation because it probably will exist for you again. But when it doesn't exist as you then the doesn't exist for you stabilizes. That's been my experience with it.

BB: *We are neither cocky nor are we afraid. That is our experience. That is how we react so long as we keep in fit Spiritual condition. It is easy to let up on the Spiritual program of action and rest on our laurels. We are headed for trouble if we do, for alcohol is a subtle foe. We are not cured of alcoholism. What we really have is a daily reprieve contingent on the maintenance of our Spiritual condition.*

Paul: This doesn't say our physical condition or mental condition, they have value, but this is putting the horse before the cart. They're talking about the maintenance of the Spiritual condition. My experience is that the highest form of maintenance of a Spiritual condition is--to *be* a Spiritual condition, not to have one. Because if I'm being this body and I'm having a Spiritual condition, that's precarious. But if I am of Spirit, then that Spirit's condition is what I am, and I'm always going to be that. It's nothing that I need to acquire or maintain, just Be.

Spirit will be its own maintenance of the Spiritual condition.

God is available at all times with no requirement necessary except for the ones that we make up.

Growing up Catholic, three pertinent points were always beaten into us, God is omnipresent, omniscient and omnipotent--God is everywhere, He knows everything and is all-powerful. If God is everywhere, how in the hell am I not running into him?

I must believe I am separate to want to know God. If I am not separate, what am I but the Being of God? If we knew that we were not separate, that would lead to the Being of God. I must believe that I am in a special somewhere to want to experience everywhere. We are everywhere. Realizing you are not in a special somewhere, the obviousness of everywhere would break over you.

How long does it take the wave to realize its the ocean when it sees its not the wave? It's located right where everywhere is, which is everywhere. But I'm thinking I'm somewhere and I'm going to go out and get an experience of everywhere, and bring it back to somewhere so that I could have the experience of everywhere as a somewhere.

Why not see that you are not a somewhere and that's everywhere. That's the freedom. **The freedom isn't *for* me, the freedom is *from* me.** If you're busy trying to get freedom for me, you're going to be buying tons of books and going to tons of retreats; you're going to be driven to get freedom, and there will be a lot of people selling it. A lot. There will be layaway plans, there will be five year subscriptions, there will be all of these accessories you have to get with the freedom to really be free. But if freedom is everywhere and you are everywhere where freedom is, to me that's being free. Even from the need to be free.

Nearing Step Eleven

Commitment and Feeling

If I was new, this would be the prayer that I would use:

Please God, grant me the ability to be convinced.

You'll save yourself a lot of trouble. This disease is chronic, it is progressive and it's life-threatening. It's going to progress whether you're drinking or not, it's still going to progress. Recovery is also progressive as long as you stay on the operating table, don't get up and don't play the doctor.

I was done (with drugs and alcohol) and before I was dead, Grace entered and led me to the program. The knowledge that I was fucked was deeply embedded in me. My practice in the beginning of *Alcoholics Anonymous* and since then has never been based on feeling.

Although a lot of the time I was happy. **For me, it had to be on the level of commitment. I could not allow the selfing to play God with my sobriety or I would not have had sobriety.** That's why commitments (a pledge to show up, usually for 6 months at a meeting to perform a service) in the program are very, very helpful. They allow a new continuum to gain traction. That opens you up for a lot of the benefits like the feeling of belonging and some self-esteem.

Commitments and being committed are very important. The ability to be convinced, if you can get it without having to get your own ass kicked is a very good thing. You can learn a whole lot from other people's mistakes. You will hear a lot of people talking about the solution from the problem best to listen to those that speak from the solution about the problem

Long-Term Sobriety

There was a woman when I was younger in *Alcoholics Anonymous* that I remember to this day. At a meeting, she came and told me that she had 10 years and she had just gone out. She got bored and she wanted to have some fun and she went out to drink and go dancing. Her assumption was that *Alcoholics Anonymous* was going to be the same as it was when she left, and it was the same as when she left, but she wasn't. When she drank, the compulsion,--that obsession, kicked in and now she wanted to drink and didn't like the meetings, which is like hating the pharmacy where your medicine is dispensed. Before she went out, she liked the meetings and she was living freed from that obsession. I've seen it happen to a lot of people who have a lot of time. When they go out they have a real difficult time getting back in. Even though they keep showing up, their state of mind has changed. Their attitude and outlook has changed. After watching this, many, many, times, some of them very close to me, this is what I've come up with. There's something about honoring the gift that you have while you have it, that will keep it really fresh for you. That form of honoring is by doing service or going to meetings and helping other people. What other forms can it take? Maybe it's just an honoring in your heart. Who knows?

Another thing I wanted to say about long-term sobriety is what it allows. It allows deep mental grooves, the ones that constitute structural predilections of the action figure to surface in the light and be allowed to reconfigure through the process of steps 6 and 7. These grooves will not be revealed (though incredibly influential) when the surface of your external life is constantly whipped into agitation by all the drama, lies, consequences, active alcoholism is. These are the energetic bonding patterns that frame us and through steps 6 & 7 they are given over to the Higher Power to do with as It will.

I find that there are a lot of dark places that won't come up until it's safe enough for them to surface. I find the years of sobriety produce that atmosphere where stuff that was running my life from the shadows are allowed to come up into the light and then seen not to be me. I find a lot of times what drives people out when they are in the program is the fear of that coming up so they act out, they get loaded and the consequential shit hits the fan. All that stuff begins to sink down again to hide for another year or two. The only real value I've seen in long-term sobriety is that it allows through time that which is hidden to be revealed. Sobriety can maintain a very favorable condition so that which ails you, that which runs you, that which haunts you, to come up and to be seen in the light.

If the consequential level is not chilled out, that stuff will never rise up but you will call it you. Instead of seeing it you will be looking from it. **Long term sobriety can offer the possibility, the right conditions so that which is "hidden" can come into the light and a transmutation of the energy that was contracted can expand.**

Step Eleven

Sought through prayer and meditation to improve our conscious contact with God, <u>as we understood Him</u>, praying only for knowledge of His will for us and the power to carry that out.
(Page 84, BB)

Once I got a flavor of this presence, of this new Power flowing, in or the sense of Spirit or Higher Power, it provoked in me, a wanting to know that Power which had saved my ass. If you live life based on self, from that seeming separation, there is a need to make contact with that which is seen as 'other' (God or the Higher Power) In separation, that which feels it is separate, believes the only way to make contact to that which is other, would be through doing, knowing and understanding. Living in the act of being identified as a self, the possibility of being that which we seek is seen as preposterous.

Prayer and Meditation, Conscious Contact

The famous statement "The seeker is the sought." - proves inscrutable. This is the major flaw of attempting to do and have yourself into an inherent condition. Taking the separation as a starting point, I would sincerely advise someone to do what they need to do to get that contact. In this circumstance, the self is the bigger God than the God it's trying to contact. **But**

it's through doing prayer and meditation that the need for prayer and meditation may come to an end as a method to reach what you already are and be seen as expressions of that which we are.

If the seeker is the sought, what would that realization do to the seeking?

When I was younger, I knew about prayer and meditation because I had been with a Spiritual teacher from India when I was 19 until 24 years old. The funny thing was, my wanting to know God was sufficient enough to keep me from drinking or using for a few years. But when I got disappointed in all that, I went out with a vengeance. When I got sober at 36, I was such a mess, (even though I knew that prayer and meditation were valuable) it took me 5 years to start meditating again on a daily basis.

I had a lot of undoing to go through. My deck needed to be reshuffled, dramatically. It took a lot of time on the operating table just to take out all the shrapnel of the wreckage. It was more than enough just to be engaged in *Alcoholics Anonymous*, going to meetings and doing service. I would use prayer quite a lot but meditation escaped me at that time. **Now I have a sense of being meditated.**

Prayer and meditation was very, very important because at that time my access to the Higher Power was still based on me and it, so circumstances and situations could cut me off from that sunlight of the Spirit very easily. Now it's much different.

The meaning of everything is determined by where we see it from. Our true role in things is aptly described in Lesson 2 in *A Course In Miracles*, **You and I give everything all the meaning it has.** This takes taking responsibility to a new level.

Remember it's not you taking responsibility, it's taking responsibility. What's taking responsibility? In recovery there seems to be 2 options, you can see life from self or you can see life from Spirit (no-thing)

One, is an interpretation that life is happening to me, and the other, life is seen as happening.

Self cannot get out of self and get into Spirit. The realization 'you are not self' reveals that you are Spirit. The experience of being out of self is the realization that you are not IN self.

Trying to get out of self, you're in self.

Self cannot get out of self. How could the product of the thought system leave the thought system? That would be the thought system. If you are looking from self, you want to get out of self. Yet self can't get out of self. What's one to do? If one entertains 'the problem is identification as a self', the warning that self cannot get out of self, will make complete sense. Getting out of self will be produced by realizing you're not a self.

How long would it take to escape an imaginary place? I'd say no time. And how much thought and effort would it take? None.

The way to get out is realizing you were never in. Ramana Maharshi, a great sage put it quite succinctly, *"There is a presupposing of a nonexistent thing and then wanting to get salvation for the non existent thing"* and "Your Spiritual practices themselves will be used to reinforce the nonexistent thing, how could they destroy it?"

Ultimately, I would hope that the idea of a Higher Power would leave the point where it's based on your understanding and you would now have a Higher Power of its own understanding.

If I have a Higher Power and it's based on my own understanding, I'm going to severely limit the effects of the Higher Power. If I am open to finding out a God of its own understanding, that's revelatory! I'm put in a position of "Don't know," and then I find out. That's much more of an emphatic form of knowledge; finding out. It has a gripping ability.

It's not convinced and unconvinced, it can produce a sense of being convinced. From the point of being the doer of the contact, what can happen to the contact? If the doer stops doing what it believes has produced the contact, he or she will experience being out of contact with the Higher Power; that's playing God. That which you are, is now seen to be that which you can be in contact with, and conversely, that which you can be out of contact with. Thats playing God. You'll notice, the out of contact experience will be the more frequent condition than the being in contact is.

The theme of the head can be easily seen in this example. When you're having a good day, how long does that last till you get agitated? If you're having a bad day, the head is heralding a lifelong depression.

The mental state is going to shrink the good and elongate the bad. Do we really want to live under that theme? No. Who the hell would like this to be the arbiter of their life? Nobody. This is the danger of what you are being put outside of yourself. The contact with what you are will be based on what you're not--self.

In seeing what you're not, what happens is, you're being what you are. Now, the 'access' is always available at all times, right where you are, with no requirement necessary except the ones you make up. It's much clearer **to be** the access instead of having to do something to **attain the access.**

When I started to meditate, I became identified as the meditator and when I missed morning meditation, I believed that my day was going to go bad. This is not peace when that which you are using to produce peace is causing anxiety around the topic of peace. This is a dilemma.If you are still in the position of being the doer, if you believe that the access to this Higher Power is based on your actions, then you will probably have very limited access. I don't want to rely on this precarious conditional access. If I am that, then I'm accessing that at all times. No matter where I am, what I'm doing, or what I'm thinking or feeling--there is an access. That, I like. That, works for me. If you really truly need something, it has to be available right where you are at all times. It can't be something that you do, it has to be something that you are.

I do not want my access to a power that I severely need, to be in the hands of my head, for that is where the problem resides, because my head will tell me I don't deserve it or I'm far away from it. A lot of times, people will have experiences where they're connected during a retreat but then they're disconnected when they're not at the retreat. I want to know that the connection is securely bonded and there's no way it could be disconnected. That works.

Let's say I believe I'm doing something that's provoking this connection with the Higher Power, it's still a form of playing God to me. What tells me if I'm doing good with my God search? Me. I would say that's the bigger God there than the God that I'm looking for. That would mean that the accessing of God would be all about "me."

* The thing is, it's not saying to make conscious contact, there already is conscious contact. You may want to improve your awareness of it, but you cannot improve conscious contact. Conscious contact is the basic state of life. *

Every experience is brought to us by conscious contact.

Consciousness is in contact.

It's going through these five senses--hearing, seeing, feeling, tasting, touching, and the 6th of seeing thoughts--like you see a bird go by with your eye, that's conscious contact.

The sense of being you is an afterthought, that arises after the contact. Yet what happens is that idea that comes after the conscious contact, that idea is assumed to be before the contact, that you are the one that's in contact. There's consciousness that is demonstrating no thought or effort to be conscious and then seemingly, "I'm the one who is conscious," and there's a lot of thought and effort to be conscious. How can I expect to become conscious, through thought and effort when consciousness exerts no thought and effort to be what it is?

If consciousness is trying to be conscious, it must believe it is something else. The mental process produces a sense of self which is taken to be you and then it presupposes that process (you) as prior to the conscious contact and you are now the one who is in conscious contact, I'm now who's in contact. Are you digesting your food? If you said that you had to go home and digest that burrito you ate last night, everyone would laugh. No, you are not doing digesting. Digestion is happening. I'm not pumping my blood. Yet we actually live in the position of being the thinker of the thoughts which is a much subtler process than any of the physical processes. This is a brain or mental process, yet from self, the idea that I am the thinker of the thoughts, is presupposed.

That's even more ludicrous than the thinking that I'm the digester of the food. To feel that one is the thinker of thoughts is a thought itself. That is one of the ultimate arrogances of self-centeredness, is the thinking you are the doer, that you actually believe that you are thinking. Thoughts just arise and they are heard. Then there's a story of who that is, which is the identification as a self and that immediately says 'I am the thinker.' It claims. That's its movement. It claims everything. It says now "I'm the thinker" yet what you actually are is the seeing of thoughts--the seeing of them. You're not the thinker of it, you are the seeing of whatever arises. You are not what's causing the arising, you are the seeing of whatever arises. Not as Paul, because that's a form of looking--that's called self-centeredness. When you take yourself to be the seer, that's called self-centeredness. What I am, is the seeing of what's going on not the seer of what's going on. That's the difference of God and self. God is seeing self is the seer. That's how everything shifts. The mental landscape of nouns and verbs is itself just verbing. There are no nouns to be found.

Remember faith is a force of mind and the way it manifests is determined by the vehicle it's put it. Faith in the thought system produces anxiety, the same faith surrendered, produces an ease and comfort in one's skin. There is freedom from the bondage of self.

Whatever it is that can improve your conscious contact, farout. I had a prayer when I first got sober because the worst time of my day was when I woke up. I'd wake up feeling like I was under the same old managerial team. I was so anxious about what was going to happen to me that day. I would say a prayer that combined the first three steps. I would say: "My name is Paul and I'm an alcoholic and drug addict. I'm powerless over alcohol and drugs, and my life has become unmanageable. I've come to believe a power greater than myself has restored me to sanity and I make a decision to turn my life and my will over to the care of a Higher Power."

I said it no matter where I was in the world, no matter who I was with; as soon as I woke up I'd say that prayer. I said it religiously and then one day after 5 years, I said it for the last time because something shifted.

A cautionary warning: Move forward at your own risk. The mental state will use whatever we do to imply the doer. This is what gives meaning to the action. Meditation can be used by the mental state to imply the meditator, praying can be used to imply the pray-er. The selfing can use what we do to produce access to the Higher Power to increase obsession with self.

After all, you may start having a sense of being meditated. You may just sense the fact that you are a prayer.

Step Twelve

Having had a Spiritual awakening as a result of theses steps we tried to carry this message to alcoholics and to practice these principles in all of our affairs.
(Page 96, BB)

Step 12 is the suggested direction one can take after having a Spiritual awakening as a result of the first 11 steps.

You can collect tons of Spiritual experiences, but it does not add up to a Spiritual awakening. Spiritual awakening is waking up to the fact that you are inherently awake.

Spiritual awakening is not an experience, how could what you are experience itself? It would have to be 'other' to experience what it is. We are relegated to only **being** it. It influences all of our experiences. Awakening is not an experience. The mind wakes up to its own nature, and how can that happen? (that which is always happening); by seeing that you're not the phantom that all the mental processes are pointing at.

Having accepted the new seat assignment, I'm going to carry the message to other people who suffer from the same condition and I'm going to practice these principles in all of my affairs. If I cannot practice these principles in all of my affairs, then I limit my affairs.

This becomes the basic theme of your life. Sometimes it's the most dominant, sometimes it seems to be less if you have kids or things like that but it's always there, that you are open and willing to be available to others.

You were in hell, someone gave you a bus ticket and a schedule and told you where to catch the bus out of the hell. Now your privilege is to return the favor. You carry the schedule, you carry the bus ticket, and you're willing to share your experience about the trip out of hell. You may even visit hell on a visa but you're not a citizen of hell anymore. You'll visit and actually feel a whole lotta heaven while you're there. You're going to pass it on to that person that if they are so inclined, so they can get out of the hell of active addiction--freedom from the tyranny of alcoholism

I was in hell. This process has taken me out of hell. It seems like a natural response to make it available to others. I see a lot of people who I feel are in the same hell that I was in. Why would I not want to inform them about the bus out of hell? Actually be there so that they can get on the bus and maybe even sit with them. Whatever lengths I have to go to to participate in people leaving hell are the same lengths others have gone to be of service to me. Passing on freely what was so freely passed on to me, the wheel of recovery rolls on.

The whole backbone of *Alcoholics Anonymous* is one alcoholic helping another.

A lot of times you are in the position where you really need to hear the message, and a lot of the time someone else is in the position where they have to carry the message. That switches.

It's a symbiotic thing going on. Meetings can be an event where a loving God expresses itself through our group conscience, as stated in tradition two.

Grace and Wisdom

You can go to meetings of recovery and maybe some of the people there are assholes, but the scent the whole room transmits is like a sweet bouquet. There's a loving presence that's expressing itself through our group conscience. Our group conscience can be one alcoholic helping another. There is Grace available. I don't ever see that Grace waning. When you participate in the dance, you get the benefit of having or sensing that Grace, in its active state, is flowing.

I was in incapable at the time of practicing these principles in all of my affairs, so I had to limit my affairs. There is great wisdom in knowing your limitations. I can't be robbing and stealing, I can't be living with people who I don't like just so that I can have a place to stay. I can't be doing a lot of the behaviors that I used to do, so a lot of my affairs came under review.

My life seemed to get a lot simpler because at that level I could participate and practice these principles. My life has expanded but I particularly like a simplicity, it works for me.

I'm not drawn to that boredom that looks exciting, now I like the excitement that looks boring.

I can practice these principles in all of my affairs. I'm willing and open to be available to others. I still go to *Alcoholics Anonymous*. I have some sponsees and I participate with people who have a desire to stay sober.

It's the lifeblood; anyone can run a perfect program from their living room but you've got to be in the mix. I go to meetings a lot because that's where I get my reminders of where I don't want to be. Before I couldn't learn from my own suffering, now I can learn from other people's experiences.

It's truly humbling being able to say that the problem doesn't exist as me. I haven't had a strong thought or feeling concerning alcohol or drugs for a long time. What need of skillful means if the end is established?!?

As an example: I'd been overseas for about three months and I hadn't attended many meetings. I came home and went to a meeting and someone asked me to be their sponsor, to help them. Afterwards, I saw my girlfriend and I told her, "Man, I don't know if I can help this person, I mean I never think of alcohol or anything." She said, "That's exactly what you have to offer." The problem does not exist for you, that's exactly what you have to offer.

I don't care about alcohol and drugs anymore, I have no interest in it. As a descriptive experience, it seems all my life I have been directed by something. In stark contrast, things are easier to see. The sense of the living is so extremely different before and after sobriety that the term taken over by a parasite feels so intimate. After relief from it, what else could you call it. Now, over the years in sobriety, I can only describe the sense I have of now is that the action figure is driven by something other than self. I will let the Higher Power be of its own understanding. Why limit it with mine.

Not knowing leads to finding out. And what I have found out is what I am not. In seeing what I'm not, I am being what I am.

That which had to be changed has been changed. All that has proved useful has been put to use. The experience is of being used. You have it by giving it away. Directed not directing. Being changed not changing. All of it being guided by a farseeing force, not a blind myopic way of looking, self-centeredness. All of this is just a byproduct of me showing up and being willing to do a few simple things. Not doing it based on feelings but bringing it to a level of commitment because one of the greatest gifts that I got was the ability to be convinced. I knew what had led me was a failed system. Deep to the core, it still resonates. That opened me up to the solution. I was willing to follow suggestions because I could not follow my own anymore. A power did for me what I could not do for myself.

Why not expand on what I cannot do for myself? If the reader is in recovery, just stay on the operating table, don't get up and don't play doctor. **See what happens!**

Infused with the Spirit. That's actually what brings life to the book, not my intellect or my reasoning but what's filled me up. That's what gives meaning to everything now. That's how I live, finding out. I'm always running into new meaning because what's giving my life meaning is not the old me.

Finding out is just a really cool way to live. With the protection of the third step, knowing you're taken care of, you can take some chances and ask for what you want. We have a statement in *Alcoholics Anonymous,* that says you have to fit yourself around circumstances instead of fitting circumstances around you.

Abandon yourself to God as you understand God. (or hopefully as God understands you) Admit your faults to Him and to your fellows, clear away the wreckage of your past, give freely of what you find and join us. We shall be with you in the fellowship of the Spirit. And you will surely meet some of us as we trudge the road of happy destiny. May God bless you and keep you until then. (page 164, BB)

You are I are the dreaming of the dream. (A Course in Miracles)

We're gonna dream ourselves out of the dream and as we do, the dream will get happier.

Thank you,
Paul

The AA Principles and Virtues

Honesty

Step 1. We admitted that we were powerless over alcohol - that our lives had become unmanageable.

Hope

Step 2. Came to believe that a power greater than ourselves could restore us to sanity.

Faith

Step 3. Made a decision to turn our will and our lives over to the care of God as we understood him.

Courage

Step 4. Made a searching and fearless moral inventory of ourselves.

Integrity

Step 5. Admitted to God, to ourselves, and to another human being the exact nature of our wrongs.

Willingness

Step 6. Were entirely ready to have God remove all these defects of character.

Humility

Step 7. Humbly asked Him to remove our shortcomings.

Brotherly Love

Step 8. Made a list of all persons we had harmed, and became willing to make amends to them all.

Justice

Step 9. Made direct amends to such people wherever possible, except when to do so would injure them or others.

Perseverance

Step 10. Continued to take personal inventory and when we were wrong promptly admitted it.

Spirituality

Step 11. Sought through prayer and meditation to improve our conscious contact with God *as we understood Him*, praying only for knowledge of his will for us and the power to carry that out.

Service

Step 12. Having had a Spiritual awakening as the result of these steps, we tried to carry this message to others, especially alcoholics and to practice these principles in all our affairs.

The Promises

---

1) We will know a new freedom & happiness.

2) We will not regret the past, nor wish to shut the door on it.

3) We will comprehend the word serenity.

4) We will know peace.

5) We will see how our experiences would benefit others.

6) That feeling of uselessness and self pity will disappear.

7) We will lose interest in selfish things.

8) Self seeking will slip away.

9) Our whole attitude and outlook on life will change.

10) Fear of people and economic insecurity will leave us.

11) We will intuitively know how to handle situations that used to baffle us.

12) We will suddenly realize that GOD is doing for us what we couldn't do for ourselves.

Keep Coming Back

Notes

Notes

Notes

Notes

Notes

Notes

Notes

Notes

Printed in Great Britain
by Amazon